WORKBOOK

VOLUME B

FOCUS ON GRAMMAR

An **INTERMEDIATE** Course for Reference and Practice

SECOND EDITION

Marjorie Fuchs

Longman

Focus on Grammar: An **Intermediate** Course for Reference and Practice
Workbook

Pearson Education, 10 Bank Street, White Plains, NY 10606

Editorial director: Allen Ascher
Executive editor: Louisa Hellegers
Director of design and production: Rhea Banker
Development editors: Angela Malovich Castro and Bill Preston
Production manager: Alana Zdinak
Managing editor: Linda Moser
Senior production editor: Virginia Bernard
Production editor: Christine Lauricella
Senior manufacturing manager: Patrice Fraccio
Manufacturing manager: David Dickey
Cover design: Rhea Banker
Text design adaptation: Rainbow Graphics
Text composition: Rainbow Graphics
Photo credits: **p. 102** Ken Biggs/Tony Stone Images; **p. 102** Tony Stone Images; **p. 131** Rubberball Productions

0–201–34677–X

6 7 8 9 10 —BAH— 08 07 06 05

CONTENTS

ABOUT THE AUTHOR

Marjorie Fuchs has taught ESL at New York City Technical College and LaGuardia Community College of the City University of New York and EFL at the Sprach Studio Lingua Nova in Munich, Germany. She holds a Master's Degree in Applied English Linguistics and a certificate in TESOL from the University of Wisconsin–Madison. She has authored or co-authored many widely used ESL textbooks, notably *On Your Way: Building Basic Skills in English, Crossroads, Top Twenty ESL Word Games, Around the World: Pictures for Practice, Families: Ten Card Games for Language Learners, Focus on Grammar: A High-Intermediate Course for Reference and Practice,* and the *Workbooks* to the *Longman Dictionary of American English,* the *Longman Photo Dictionary, The Oxford Picture Dictionary,* and the *Vistas* series.

UNIT

22

ADJECTIVES AND ADVERBS

❶ SPELLING

Write the adjectives and adverbs.

Adjectives	Adverbs
1. quick	quickly
2. *nice.*	nicely
3. fast	*Fast.*
4. good	*well.*
5. *dangerous*	dangerously
6. beautiful	*beautifully*
7. *hard.*	hard
8. safe	*safely*
9. *occasional.*	occasionally
10. *happy*	happily
11. *sudden.*	suddenly
12. careful	*carefully*
13. angry	*angrily.*
14. *unfortunate*	unfortunately

❷ WORD ORDER

Emily is telling her friend about her new apartment. Put the words in the correct order to make sentences and complete the conversation.

A: Congratulations! (heard about / I / apartment / new / your).

    1.   I heard about your new apartment.

B: Thank you! (news / good / fast / travels)!

    2. _____

(continued on next page)

A: What's it like?

B: (five / rooms / has / it / large),

3. _____

and (building / it's / large / a / very / in).

4. _____

A: How's the rent?

B: (too / it's / bad / not).

5. _____

A: And what about the neighborhood?

B: (seems / quiet / it / pretty).

6. _____

But (landlord / the / very / speaks / loudly).

7. _____

A: How come?

B: (well / doesn't / he / hear).

8. _____

A: Well, that doesn't really matter. (it / decision / was / hard / a)?

9. _____

B: Not really. We liked the apartment, and besides (quickly / had to / we / decide).

10. _____

There were a lot of other people interested in it.

A: Oh, no! Look at the time! (I / leave / now / have to).

11. _____

(luck / with / good / apartment / new / your)!

12. _____

B: Thanks. So long.

❸ ADJECTIVE OR ADVERB

Emily wrote a letter to a friend. Complete the letter. Use the correct form of the words in parentheses ( ).

Dear Lauren,

I'm _____totally_____ exhausted! James and I finished moving into our new
    1. (total)
apartment today. It was a lot of _____ work, but everything worked
    2. (hard)
out _____.
    3. (good)
The apartment looks _____. It's _____
    4. (nice)   **5. (extreme)**
_____. The only problem is with the heat. I always feel
6. (comfortable)
_____. We'll have to speak to the landlord about it. He seems
    7. (cold)
_____ _____.
    8. (pretty)   **9. (friendly)**
People tell me that the neighborhood is very _____. That's
    10. (safe)
_____ _____ because I get home _____
  11. (real)   **12. (important)**   **13. (late)**
from work. I hate it when the streets are _____ _____
    14. (complete)   **15. (empty)**
like they were in our old neighborhood. Shopping is _____, too.
    16. (good)
We can get to all the stores very _____. The bus stop is
    17. (easy)
_____ the apartment, and the buses run _____.
  18. (near)   **19. (frequent)**
Why don't you come for a visit? It would be _____ to see you.
    20. (wonderful)
I haven't seen you since our wedding. Please write.

Love,
Emily

4 *-ED* OR *-ING* ADJECTIVES

Emily and James are going to rent a video. Circle the correct adjective form to complete these brief movie reviews from a video guide.

At Home at the Movies

23

BILLY BUDD Based on Herman Melville's powerful and (1. fascinated / fascinating) novel, this well-acted, well-produced film will leave you (2. disturbed / disturbing).

THE BURNING There's nothing (3. entertained / entertaining) about this 1981 horror film that takes place in a summer camp. You'll be (4. disgusted / disgusting) by all the blood in this story of revenge.

CHARIOTS OF FIRE Made in England, this is an (5. inspired / inspiring) story about two Olympic runners. Wonderfully acted.

COMING HOME Jon Voight plays the role of a (6. paralyzed / paralyzing) war veteran in this (7. moved / moving) drama about the effects of war. Powerful.

THE COMPETITION Well-acted love story about two pianists who fall in love while competing for the top prize in a concert. You'll be (8. moved / moving). Beautiful music.

FOLLOW ME QUIETLY A (9. frightened / frightening) thriller about a mentally (10. disturbed / disturbing) man who kills people when it rains. Not for the weak-hearted.

THE GRADUATE Director Mike Nichols won an Academy Award for this funny, but (11. touched / touching) look at a young man trying to figure out his life after college.

THE GREEN WALL Mario Robles Godoy's photography is absolutely (12. astonished / astonishing) in this story of a young Peruvian family. In Spanish with English subtitles.

INVASION OF THE BODY SNATCHERS One of the most (13. frightened / frightening) science fiction movies ever made. You won't be (14. bored / boring).

WEST SIDE STORY No matter how many times you see this classic musical, you will never be (15. disappointed / disappointing). The story, based on Shakespeare's *Romeo and Juliet*, is (16. touched / touching), and the music by Leonard Bernstein is delightful and (17. excited / exciting).

WILBUR AND ORVILLE: THE FIRST TO FLY This is an (18. entertained / entertaining) biography of the two famous Wright brothers. Good for kids, too. They'll learn a lot without ever being (19. bored / boring).

ADJECTIVES:
COMPARATIVES AND EQUATIVES

1 SPELLING: REGULAR AND IRREGULAR COMPARATIVES

Write the comparative forms of the adjectives.

Adjective	Comparative
1. slow	slower
2. expensive	more expensive
3. hot	hotter
4. big	bigger
5. good	better
6. difficult	more difficult
7. pretty	prettier
8. beautiful	more beautiful
9. bad	worse
10. long	longer
11. far →	farer. *farther.*
12. careful	carefuller. *more carefull*
13. dangerous	more dangerous
14. early	earlier
15. terrible	more terrible
16. wide	wider
17. noisy	noisier
18. comfortable	more comfortable
19. wet	wetter
20. cheap	cheaper

② THE COMPARATIVE FORM

*Complete this conversation between two neighbors who meet in a department store. Use the correct form of the words in parentheses ( ). Use **than** when necessary.*

EMILY: Amy!

AMY: Emily! What are you doing here?

EMILY: I'm trying to buy a microwave oven. Do you know if the small ones are really any

_____worse than_____ the _____larger_____ ones?
    1. (bad)   **2. (large)**

AMY: I'm not sure, but I think they're _____slower_____. Are you getting
                3. (slow)

things for your new apartment?

EMILY: Yes. James and I moved in last Friday.

AMY: How do you like it?

EMILY: It's great. It's _____bigger than_____ our old one. It has an extra
           4. (big)

bedroom. And it faces the back, so it's _____quieter_____. You can't
                5. (quiet)

hear the traffic at all.

AMY: How's the rent?

EMILY: That's the only problem. It's a little _____more expensive_____.
                6. (expensive)

AMY: But it's _____cheaper than_____ a house.
      7. (cheap)

EMILY: That's true. The location is _____better_____ for us, too. Everything
                8. (good)

is _____more convenient_____—shopping, schools.
      9. (convenient)

AMY: Isn't it _____farther_____ from your office, though?
      10. (far)

EMILY: Yes. But I take the express bus and get there even _____faster than_____
                11. (fast)

before. Besides, I can relax on the bus, so it's _____more comfortable_____.
                12. (comfortable)

AMY: That's good. Emily, do you know the time?

EMILY: Yes. It's 4:35.

AMY: Oh! It's _____later than_____ I thought! I've got to run. Good luck with
           13. (late)

your new apartment.

EMILY: Thanks! I'll give you a call when we get _____settled_____. Maybe we
                14. (settled)

could have lunch together.

AMY: Sounds great.

3 THE COMPARATIVE FORM

Look at this chart comparing two microwave *ovens. Complete the sentences, using the words in parentheses ( ). Also, fill in the blanks with the brand—**X** or **Y**.*

hornos

Better ←——→ Worse

peso

Brand	Price	Size (cubic ft.)	Weight (lbs.)	Defrosting	Heating	Speed	Noise
					Calorias	Velocidad	Ruido
X	$181	0.5	31	●	○	◐	○
Y	$147	0.6	36	◐	●	●	◐

1. Brand _____X_____ is _____more expensive than_____ Brand _____Y_____ .
   (expensive)

2. Brand _____Y_____ is _____cheaper than_____ Brand _____x_____ .
   (cheap)

3. Brand _____Y_____ is _____larger_____ Brand _____x_____ .
   (large)

4. Brand _____Y_____ is _____heavier_____ Brand _____x_____ .
   (heavy)

5. For defrosting food, Brand _____x_____ is _____more efficient than_____
   (efficient)
   Brand _____Y_____ .

6. For heating food, Brand _____Y_____ is _____more effective than_____
   (effective)
   Brand _____x_____ .

7. Brand _____Y_____ is _____faster than_____ Brand _____x_____ .
   (fast)

8. Brand _____x_____ is _____noisier than_____ Brand _____Y_____ .
   (noisy)

9. In general, Brand _____Y_____ seems _____better than_____
   (good)
   Brand _____x_____ .

10. In general, Brand _____x_____ seems _____worse than_____
    (bad)
    Brand _____Y_____ .

4 COMPARISONS WITH *AS . . . AS*

*Read the facts about Los Angeles and New York City. Complete the
sentences. Use the words in parentheses ( ) with* **as . . . as** *or*
not as . . . as.

	Los Angeles	**New York City**
Total population	3,555,638	7,380,906
Population per square mile	7,572	23,894
Land area	469.3 square miles	308.9 square miles
Average temperature	57.2°F (January)	31.8°F (January)
	74.1°F (July)	76.7°F (July)
Sunny days	143	107
Annual rainfall	12″	40″
Average wind speed	7.4 mph	9.4 mph

1. In population, Los Angeles is _____ not as big as _____ New York.
   (big)

2. Los Angeles _not as crowded as_ New York.
   (crowded)

3. In land area, New York is _not as big as_ Los Angeles.
   (big)

4. In the winter, Los Angeles is _not as cold as_ New York.
   (cold)

5. In the summer, Los Angeles is almost _not as hot as_ New York.
   (hot)

6. Los Angeles is _not as wet as_ New York.
   (wet)

7. Los Angeles is _not as windy as_ New York.
   (windy)

8. New York is _not as sunny as_ Los Angeles.
   (sunny)

5 CAUSE AND EFFECT WITH TWO COMPARATIVES

Research suggests that there is a connection between the crime rate in U.S. cities and certain other factors. Read the information. Rewrite the information, using two comparatives.

[handwritten annotations: Investigacion, Sugerir, indice or porcentaje]

1. When cities are large, they usually have high crime rates.

   The larger the city, the higher the crime rate.

2. When cities are small, they usually have low crime rates.

   [handwritten: bajo] The smaller the city, the lower (the) crime rate.

3. When cities have warm climates, the police are usually busy.

   The warmer climate city, the busier the police.

4. When the weather is cold, there is usually a great number of robberies. *[handwritten: Robos]*

   The colder the weater, The greater the number of robberies

5. When the police force is large, the city is usually violent.

   The larger the police force, the more violent the city

6. When it's late in the day, the number of car thefts is usually high. *[handwritten: Robos]*

   The later in the day the higher the number of car thefts.

7. When the unemployment rate is high, the crime rate is usually also high.

   The Higher unemployment rate, the higher the crime rate.

8. When the population is mobile (people move from place to place), the city is usually dangerous.

   The more mobile the population the more dangerous the city

9. When communities are organized, neighborhoods are usually safe.

   The more oganized the community, The safer the neighborhoods.

6 THE COMPARATIVE TO EXPRESS CHANGE

Look at these graphs. They show trends in the capital of the United States, Washington, D.C. Make statements about the trends. Use the comparative form of the adjectives in parentheses ( ).

1. Population

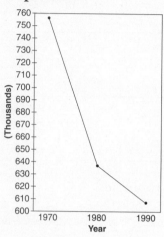

The population of Washington, D.C.,

is getting smaller and smaller.
(small)

2. Population Per Square Mile

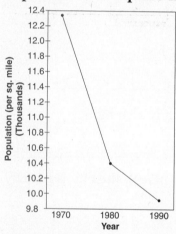

Washington, D.C., is getting less and less crowded
(crowded)

3. Unemployment

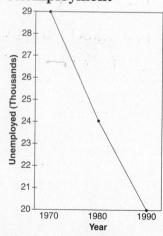

The number of unemployed people

is getting lower and lower.
(low)
bajo

Renta Ingresos utilidades.

4. Personal Income

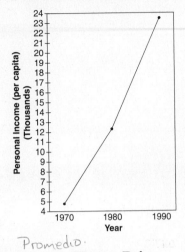

is getting

Personal income <u>is getting higher and higher</u>
(high)

Promedio.

5. Average House Price

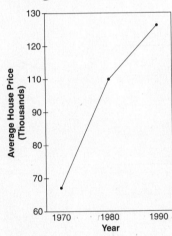

Homes <u>is getting more and more expensive.</u>
(expensive)

---

7 PERSONALIZATION

Tendencias

Write about trends in your country or city.

1.   My city is getting more and more crowded.

2.   My city is more and more beautifull than other years.

3.   My city has more and more shopping center.

4.   My city has more and more population

5.   My city is clearer and clearer

24 ADJECTIVES: SUPERLATIVES

1 SPELLING: REGULAR AND IRREGULAR SUPERLATIVES

Write the superlative form of the adjectives.

Adjective	Superlative
1. nice	the nicest
2. funny	the funniest
3. big	the biggest
4. wonderful	the most wonderful
5. good	The best
6. bad	the worst
7. happy	The happiest
8. important	The most important
9. warm	the warmest
10. interesting	the most Interesting
11. far	the farthest
12. intelligent	the most Intelligent
13. slow	the slowest
14. expensive	the most expensive

2 THE SUPERLATIVE

*Look at the newspaper ads for three cameras on the next page and complete the conversation between a customer and salesclerk. Use the superlative form (**the . . . -est** or **the most / the least**) of the adjectives in parentheses ( ). Also, write the name of the camera they are talking about.*

CLERK: Can I help you?

CUSTOMER: Yes. I'm looking for a camera for my daughter. I want to spend between $40

and $100. What's _____the best_____ camera you have in that

                1. (good)

price range?

CLERK: Well, there are three cameras I can show you. __the least expensive__

                                         2. (expensive)

is the _____Funji_____. It sells for only $39.98.

          3.

CUSTOMER: And how much is __the most expensive__?

                        4. (expensive)

CLERK: That's the _____Minon_____. It's on sale for $99.98, and I can

                5.

guarantee that that's _____the lowest_____ price in town. It usually

                        6. (low)

sells for $130.00.

CUSTOMER: How are the three cameras different?

CLERK: Well, the _____Minon_____ is _____smallest_____.

                7.   **8. (small)**

It can fit right inside your pocket.

CUSTOMER: That sounds good. I guess it's _____lightest_____, too.

                              9. (light)

CLERK: No, not really. It's the only one of the three with a zoom lens. That makes it

__the most powerfull__ because it brings the picture closer to you.

      10. (powerful)

But it also makes the camera __the heaviest__. It weighs 14

                              11. (heavy)

ounces. The other two weigh only 10 ounces.

CUSTOMER: I see. What about flashes?

CLERK: All three come with a built-in flash. But the _____Minon_____

                                    12.

(continued on next page)

turns on automatically when there isn't enough light. That makes it

the most convenient. Oh, you should also know about a special

13. (convenient)

feature of the ___Rikon___. It has what's called "red-eye

14.

reduction." That means that when you take a picture of a person and use the

flash, the person's eyes won't look red. That's often a problem when you use a

flash.

CUSTOMER: Oh, that's probably _the least important_ feature in my daughter's

15. (important)

case. She only takes pictures of flowers and trees!

❸ THE SUPERLATIVE

Complete these world facts. Use the superlative form of the correct adjectives from the box.

busy	expensive	fast	large	popular	small
deep	far	heavy	long	slow	tall

1. Russia is 6,590,876 square miles (17,070,289 square kilometers). It's

the largest country in the world.

2. The Republic of Maldives is only 115 square miles (294 square kilometers). It's

The smallest country in the world.

3. The Pacific Ocean has a depth of 13,215 feet (4,028 meters). It's _the deepest_

ocean in the world.

4. The Petronas Tower in Chicago has 110 floors with a height of 1,482 feet (452 meters).

It's _the tallest_ building in the world.

5. The Seikan Tunnel in Japan stretches for 33.49 miles (53.9 kilometers). It's

the longest tunnel in the world.

6. The planet Pluto is 3,666 million miles from the sun. It's _the farthest_

planet from the sun.

7. In one year, O'Hare airport in Chicago serves more than 66,000,000 passengers. It's

the busiest airport in the world.

8. France gets more than 61,500,000 visitors a year. It's _the most popular_ vacation destination in the world.

9. The cost of living in Tokyo is very high. In fact, Tokyo is _the most expensive_ city in the world.

10. The cheetah (an animal in the cat family) runs 70 mph. It's _the fastest_ animal in the world.

11. The garden snail moves at a speed of only 0.03 mph. It's _the slowest_ animal in the world.

12. The African elephant weighs 14,432 pounds (7,000 kilograms). It's _the heaviest_ land animal in the world.

25 ADVERBS: EQUATIVES, COMPARATIVES, SUPERLATIVES

1 SPELLING: REGULAR AND IRREGULAR COMPARATIVE AND SUPERLATIVE FORMS OF ADVERBS

Write the comparative and superlative form of the adverbs.

Adverb	Comparative	Superlative
1. quickly	more quickly	the most quickly
2. fast	faster	the fastest
3. beautifully	more beautifully	the most beautifully
4. soon	sooner	soonest
5. dangerously	more dangerously	the most dangerously
6. well	better	the best
7. early	earlier	the earliest
8. carefully	more carefully	the most carefully
9. badly	worse	the worst
10. far	farther	the farthest

2 THE COMPARATIVE FORM OF ADVERBS

*Here is what basketball players from two teams said about the game they played. Complete their comments. Use the correct form of the words in parentheses ( ). Use **than** when necessary.*

GEORGE: The other team played well, but we played much

_____ better _____. That's why we got the results
　　　　　　　1. (good)

we did.

* * * * * *

BOB: We played ___ harder than ___ our opponents. We

　　 merecimos　　　**2. (hard)**

deserved to win, and we did.

　 /dizôrv/

ALEX: It wasn't a great game for me. I moved _____slower than_____

3. (slow)

usual because of my bad ankle. In a few weeks I should be able to run

_____faster_____. I hope that'll help the team.

4. (fast)

* * * * * *

RICK: Our shooting was off today. We missed too many baskets. We need to shoot

_____more accurately_____ if we want to win.

5. (accurate)

* * * * * *

LARRY: I was surprised by how well they played. They played

_____more aggressively than_____ they've played in a long time. We couldn't beat

6. (aggressive)

them.

* * * * * *

ELVIN: I'm disappointed. We've been playing a lot _____worse than_____ our

7. (bad)

opponents this season. We really have to try to concentrate much

_____better_____ in order to break this losing streak.

8. (good)

* * * * * *

RANDY: Team spirit was very strong. We played a lot _____more successfully_____

9. (successful)

together, and it paid off.

* * * * * *

DENNIS: Of course I'm happy with the results. But if we want to keep it up, we have to

practice _____more seriously_____ and _____more regular than_____

10. (serious) 11. (regular)

we have been. I think we got lucky today.

Now write the names of the players under the correct team.

Winning Team	**Losing Team**
George	Alex
Bob	Rick
Randy	Larry
Dennis	Elvin

❸ COMPARISON OF ADVERBS WITH *AS . . . AS*

Look at these track-and-field records for five athletes. Then complete the statements about them. Use the cues and **(not) as . . . as**.

Event	100 Meter Run	High Jump	Discus Throw
Athlete A	9 min. 36 sec.	7 ft. 9³/4 in.	217 ft. 2 in.
Athlete B	10 min. 02 sec	6 ft. 8¹/4 in.	233 ft.
Athlete C	9 min. 59 sec.	7 ft. 10 in.	220 ft. 6 in.
Athlete D	10 min. 02 sec.	7 ft. 10 in.	233 ft.
Athlete E	10 min. 18 sec.	7 ft. 11 in.	233 ft. 1 in.

1. Athlete B _____ didn't run as fast as _____ Athlete A.
   (run / fast)
2. Athlete B _____ run as fast as _____ Athlete D.
   (run / fast)
3. Athlete C _____ jumped as high as _____ Athlete D.
   (jump / high)
4. Athlete A _____ didn't jump as high as _____ Athlete E.
   (jump / high)
5. Athlete C _____ didn't throw the discus as far as _____ Athlete E.
   (throw the discus / far)
6. Athlete D _____ threw the discus as far as _____ Athlete B.
   (throw the discus / far)
7. All in all, Athlete B _____ didn't do as well as _____ Athlete D.
   (do / good)
8. All in all, Athlete A _____ didn't compete as successfully as _____ Athlete C.
   (compete / successful)

❹ THE COMPARATIVE AND THE SUPERLATIVE OF ADVERBS

Look at the chart in Exercise 3. Complete the statements with the correct form of the words in parentheses ( ). Use **than** *when necessary. Fill in the blanks with the correct athlete—A, B, C, D, or E.*

1. Athlete B ran _____ faster than _____ Athlete _E_, but Athlete _A_ ran
   (fast)
   _____ the fastest _____ of all.
   (fast)
2. Athlete _E_ ran _____ the slowest _____. He ran _____ slower than _____
   (slow)   **(slow)**
   all the other players.
3. Athlete A jumped _____ higher than _____ Athlete _B_.
   (high)
4. Athlete _E_ jumped _____ highest _____ of all five athletes.
   (high)

5. Athletes B and D didn't throw the discus __farther____than__ Athlete _E_.

6. Athlete _E_ threw the discus _The fasthest_ **(far)** .

7. Athlete _E_ won in two categories. He performed _the best_ **(good)** .

desempeñar
ejecutar.

5 THE COMPARATIVE OF ADVERBS TO EXPRESS CHANGE

Read about these athletes. Then make a statement about each. Use the correct form of the words in the box.

(exacto, preciso) /ákya-it/

accurate	far	frequent	hard	slow
dangerous	fast	graceful	high	

/fɑr/
└ agraciado, Elegante.

1. Last month Lisa ran a mile in twelve minutes. This month she's running a mile in eight minutes.

   She's running faster and faster.

2. Last month she ran three times a week. This month she's running every day.

   She's running more and more frequently

3. Last month Josh only threw the ball ten yards. This month he's throwing it thirteen yards.

   He's throwing the ball farther and farther.

4. Last month when Jennifer shot baskets, she got only five balls in. Now when she shoots baskets, she gets at least eight balls in.

   Lanzando
   (Precisamente or exacto)
   She's shooting more and more accurately

5. Six months ago Mike jumped only four and a half feet. Now he's jumping almost six feet.
   casi

   He's jumping higher and higher.

6. Matt used to run an eight-minute mile. These days he can only run a ten-minute mile.

   He's running slower and slower
   /eski/

7. The ice-skating team of Sonia and Boris used to get four points for artistic impression.
   Calificando
   These days they are scoring more than five points.

   They're skating more and more gracefully

(continued on next page)

8. The members of the basketball team used to practice two hours a day. Now they're practicing three hours a day.

They're practicing harder and harder.

9. Jason drives a race car. Last year he had two accidents. This year he's already had five accidents.

carrera

He's driving more and more dangerously.

6 EDITING

diario - revista - boletín

Read Luisa's exercise journal. Find and correct seven mistakes in the use of adverbs. The first mistake is already corrected.

4/14/01

than
I just completed my run. I'm running much longer ~~that~~

before. Today I ran for thirty minutes without getting out of

slower
breath. I'm glad I decided to run more ~~slow~~. The more slowly

faster
I run, the ~~farthest~~ I can go. I'm really seeing progress.

frequently
Because I'm enjoying it, I run more and more ~~frequent~~. And

the more often I do it, the longer and farther I can go. I

quickly
really believe that running helps me feel better more ~~quick~~

than other forms of exercise. I'm even sleeping better than

before!

I'm thinking about running in the next marathon. I may

as
not run as fast ~~than~~ younger runners, but I think I can run

longer
~~long~~ and farther. We'll see!

GERUNDS:
SUBJECT AND OBJECT

1 GERUNDS AS SUBJECT AND AS OBJECT

*Complete this article in a health magazine. Use the gerund form of the
verbs in parentheses ( ).*

KICK UP YOUR HEELS!

In recent years ___dancing___ has become a

1. (dance)

very popular way to stay in shape. In addition to its

health benefits, it also has social advantages. "I enjoy

___go___ out and ___meeting___

2. (go)   **3. (meet)**

new people," says Diana Romero, a 28-year-old word processor.

"___sitting___ all day at a computer isn't healthy. After work I

4. (Sit)

need to move." And Diana isn't alone on the dance floor. Many people

who dislike ___running___, ___lifting___ weights, or

5. (run)   **6. (lift)**

___doing___ sit-ups are swaying to the beat of the swing, salsa,

7. (do)

and rumba. So, if you are looking for an enjoyable way to build muscles

and friendships, consider ___taking___ a spin on one of the

8. (take)

many studio dance floors that are opening up in cities across the

country. "___Exercising___ can be fun," says Sandra Carrone, owner

9. (Exercise)

of Studio Two-Step. So, quit ___wasting___ time, grab a partner,

10. (waste)

and kick up your heels!

---

② GERUNDS AS SUBJECT AND AS OBJECT

Look at the results of this questionnaire on four people's likes and dislikes. Then complete the sentences below with appropriate gerunds.

Key: **+** = enjoy
✓ = don't mind
– = dislike

	Diana	Hector	Minh	Amy
1. dance	+	–	+	–
2. walk	+	+	+	+
3. do sit-ups	–	+	–	–
4. play tennis	–	✓	+	–
5. jog (Empujar)	–	+	✓	–
6. lift weights	✓	✓	–	+

Alzar. Levantar
(lift)

1. Hector is the only one who enjoys _____ doing sit-ups _____.

2. Minh doesn't like ___ lifting weights ___, but Diana doesn't mind it.

3. Minh really enjoys ___ playing tennis ___, but Diana and Amy both dislike
   ambos
   it.

4. Diana enjoys ___ Dancing ___, but Amy really dislikes it.

5. ___ doing sit ups ___ is the activity that people most disliked.

6. Half of the people don't mind ___ lifting weights ___.

7. ___ Dancing ___ is an activity that half of the people enjoy.

8. ___ Walking ___ is the only activity that all four enjoy.

9. Diana and Minh are going to go ___ Dancing ___ together at the Two-
   Step Studio. They both enjoy it.

10. Minh doesn't mind ___ jogging ___.

11. Amy and Diana dislike ___ Playing tennis ___.

12. They also dislike ___ Jogging ___.

❸ GERUNDS AFTER CERTAIN VERBS

Sandra Carrone is having a dance party at her studio. Complete the summary sentences with the appropriate verbs from the box and use the gerund form of the verbs in parentheses ( ).

negar revisar

admit	deny	enjoy	mind	regret
consider	dislike	keep	~~quit~~	suggest

1. **MINH:** Would you like a cup of coffee?

   DIANA: No, thanks. I haven't had coffee in five years.

   Diana _____quit drinking_____ coffee five years ago.
   (drink)

2. **OSCAR:** Oh, they're playing a tango. Would you like to dance?

   RIKA: No, thanks. It's not my favorite dance.

   Rika _____ the tango.
   (do)

3. **AMY:** Do you often come to these dance parties?

   MARIA: Yes. It's a good opportunity to dance with a lot of different partners.

   Maria ____enjoy dancing____ with different partners.
   (dance)

4. **LAURA:** I don't know how to do the cha-cha. Could you show me?

   BILL: OK. Just follow me.

   Bill doesn't ____deny teaching____ Laura the cha-cha.
   (teach)

5. **DIANA:** This is a difficult dance. How did you learn it?

   MINH: I practiced it again and again.

   Minh ____mind practicing____ the dance.
   (practice)

6. **VERA:** Ow. You stepped on my toe!

   LUIS: No, I didn't!

   Luis _____ on Vera's toe.
   (step)

7. **BILL:** Are you going to take any more classes?

   LAURA: I'm not sure. I haven't decided yet. Maybe.

   Laura is ____suggest taking____ more dance classes.
   (take)

(continued on next page)

8. **DIANA:** I really love dancing.

   MINH: Me too. I'm sorry I didn't start years ago. It's a lot of fun.

   Minh _____ dance lessons sooner.
   (not begin)

9. **BILL:** Why don't we go out for coffee after class next week?

   LAURA: OK. I'd like that.

   Bill _____Consider going_____ out after class.
   (go)

10. **MINH:** You look tired.

    LAURA: I *am* tired. I think this will be the last dance for me.

    Laura _____Admit feeling_____ tired.
    (feel)

❹ PERSONALIZATION

*Look at the chart in Exercise 2. How do you feel about the six activities in the chart? Write sentences using **enjoy**, **don't mind**, or **dislike**. If you have never done an activity, begin your sentence with:* **I (don't) think I would enjoy. . . .**

1. _____I enjoy dance._____
2. _____I Enjoy walk_____
3. _____I don't mind do sit-ups_____
4. _____I don't have played tennis_____
5. _____I dislike jog_____
6. _____I dislike lift weights._____

GERUNDS AFTER PREPOSITIONS

① PREPOSITIONS AFTER CERTAIN VERBS AND ADJECTIVES

Complete the chart with the correct preposition. You will use some prepositions more than once.

about	for	in	of	on	to

1. look forward _____to_____

2. be tired _____of_____

3. be used _____to_____

4. insist _____on_____

5. believe ~~about~~ in

6. apologize for or to
   disculparse.

7. approve ~~on~~ of
   Aprobar, consentir.

8. succeed ~~to~~ in
   suceder, tener exito

9. be worried ~~on~~ about

10. be opposed _____to_____
    oponerse, Hacer frente a

② GERUNDS AFTER PREPOSITIONS

consejo

Read these conversations that take place at a student council meeting. Complete the summary sentences. Use the expressions in Exercise 1 and the gerund form of the verbs in parentheses ( ).

Sumario. Resumen.

1. **KYLE:** Where were you? It's 7:30. Our meeting started at 7:00.

   JOHN: I know. I'm sorry.

   John _____apologized for coming_____ late.
   (come)

(continued on next page)

2. **Matt:** I have some good news. We've reached our goal. Since our last meeting, we've
collected more than 100 student signatures in favor of going on strike.

akanzado.
socegado, recogido.
firmas
ir huelga
→ golpear asestar.

The students _succed in collecting_ more than 100 signatures.
(collect)

3. **Amy:** I'm not so sure it's a good idea to strike.

John: Final exams are in a few weeks. It'll be a problem if we miss classes.

John _Is worried about missing_ classes.
(miss)

4. **Amy:** I don't know. We've always solved our problems with the administration before.

John: That's true. In the past they've always listened to us.

These students _are used to working_ together with the administration.
(work)

5. **Amy:** I'm against striking. We should talk to the administration again.

John: I agree. That's the best way to solve this problem.

Amy and John _believe in talking_ to the administration again.
(talk)

6. **Matt:** We keep asking the administration for a response. They've said nothing.

Eva: That's right. We've had enough. We don't want to wait any more.

These students _are tired of waiting_ for an answer.
(wait)

7. **John:** Can we give this decision a little more time?

Matt: No, I'm sorry. We really *have to* reach a decision today.

alcanzar.

Matt _Insists of reaching_ a decision immediately.
(reach)

8. **Matt:** Let's take a vote. All those in favor of going on strike raise your hand. . . . OK.

That's 10 for and 2 against. We'll recommend a strike to the student body.

The student council _approves of having_ a strike.
(have)

9. **Eva:** Only two people voted no.

Only two council members _are oppose to going_ on strike.
(go)

10. **Amy:** I don't know about you, but I'll be glad when all this is over.

John: I know what you mean. I'll be happy when things return to normal.

Amy and John are _looking forward to returning_ to their normal activities.
(return)

❸ GERUNDS AFTER PREPOSITIONS

Complete this editorial in the student newspaper. Use the gerund form of the appropriate verbs from the box.

be	~~get~~	hear	~~miss~~	strike
fire	~~go~~	make	permit	try

Yesterday the student council voted 10 to 2 in favor of _____going_____ on strike. By __striking__ **1.**, they hope to reverse the **2.** administration's decision to fire two popular teachers. The students are very much against __firing__ teachers because of their **3.** political views. They strongly believe in __permitting__ the free expression of all **4.** opinions. They feel that teachers, as well as students, should be able to say what they want without ____being____ afraid of the **5.** administration's reaction.

If the student council succeeds in __getting__ student support, the **6.**

strike will begin on Tuesday. Not all students, however, support the idea of a strike. Many are afraid of ___Missing___ classes just a **7.** few weeks before exam time. They haven't given up ___trying___ to solve the **8.** problem with the administration. Other students haven't made up their minds yet. Which side are you on? Before ___Making___ a final decision, we **9.** suggest that you attend the students' meeting on Monday at 4:00. After ___hearing___ **10.** both sides, it may be easier to make a decision.

ambos

❹ PERSONALIZATION

How do you feel about school? Complete these sentences by adding a preposition and a gerund.

1. I'm looking forward __to finishing the English course__

2. I'm a little worried _____

3. I've gotten used _____

4. I sometimes get tired __of listening Misic in English__

INFINITIVES AFTER CERTAIN VERBS

① INFINITIVES AFTER CERTAIN VERBS

Read this exchange of letters in an advice column. Use the cues to complete the letters. Choose the correct tense of the first verb and use the infinitive form of the second verb.

Dear Gabby,

I've known John for two years. Last month after a lot of discussion, we

_____ decided to get _____ married. Since then our relationship has
1. (decide / get) *critica*
malo
been a nightmare. John criticizes me for every little thing, and we are constantly
pesadilla

fighting. I _____ want to see _____ a marriage counselor, but John
2. (want / see) *matrimonia\consejero*

_____ refuses to go _____ with me. Last night he even _____ *aun*
3. (refuse / go)

_____ threatened to end _____ the relationship if I mention the idea of
4. (threaten / end)
counseling again. *amenaza*

I don't understand what's going on. We used to get along great. I still love

John, but I _____ hesitate to take _____ the next step.
5. (hesitate / take)
What should I do? *No Atreverse, vacilar*

One Step Out the Door

> *Dear One Step Out the Door,*
>
> I've heard your story many times before. You're right to be concerned. John
>
> _parece /sem/_
> _____Seems to be_____ afraid of getting married. As soon as
> **6. (seem / be)** _eρsɑrσε_
>
> you got engaged, he ___attempted to create___ distance by fighting
> _intentar, tratar de_ **7. (attempt / create)** _crear_
>
> with you. I agree that counseling is a good idea if the two of you really
> _estar de acuerdo_
> ___Intend to stay___ together. Maybe each of you
> **8. (intend / stay)** _c/u ud._
>
> ___needs to speak___ to a counselor separately before going to
> **9. (need / speak)**
>
> one together. It's possible that John __will agree to go__ alone
> **10. (agree / go)**
>
> to discuss some of his fears. _/fir/_
> _(miedo, temores)_
>
> *Gabby*

---

2 VERB + INFINITIVE OR VERB + OBJECT + INFINITIVE

Read some conversations that take place between men and women in relationships. Complete the summary statements.

1. **SHE:** I *really* think you should see a therapist.

   HE: I'm not going to.

   incitar.
   She urged _him to see a therapist._

   He refused _to see a therapist._

2. **HE:** You do the dishes.

   SHE: No, you do the dishes.

   He didn't want _to do the dishes_

   She wanted _him to do the dishes._

3. **HE:** Don't forget to buy some milk.

   SHE: OK. I'll get some on the way home.

   /rimind/
   He reminded _her to buy some milk_
   recordo.
   She agreed _to buy some milk on the way home._

(continued on next page)

4. **SHE:** Will you do me a favor? Could you drive me to my aunt's?

HE: OK.

She asked _Him to drive her to her aunt's_

He agreed _to drive her to her aunt's_

5. **SHE:** Would you like to have dinner at my place Friday night?

HE: Uhm. I'm not sure. Uhm. I guess so. | Me imagino que si.

She invited _him to have dinner at her place_

He hesitated _to have dinner at her place_
(vacilar, atreverse)

6. **SHE:** Will you give me your answer tomorrow?

HE: Yes, I will. That's a promise.

She wants _him to give her his answer_

He promised _To give her his answer._

7. **SHE:** Would you like me to cut your hair? It's really long.

HE: Oh, OK.

She offered _to cut his hair_

He is going to <u>allow</u> _Permitir Her to cut his hair_

8. **SHE:** It's 8:00. I thought you said you'd be home at 7:00.

HE: No. I always get home at 8:00.

She expected _him to be home at 7:00_

He expected _to be home at 8:00_

9. **HE:** Could you call me before you leave the office?

SHE: I was going to, but I forgot.

He would like _her to call him before she leaves the office_

She intended _to call him before she left the office_

3 EDITING

Read this journal entry. Find and correct six mistakes in the use of infinitives. The first mistake is already corrected.

Friday, October 15

Gabby answered my letter! She advised us̶e̶ to go to counseling separately. I don't know if John will agree going, but I'm going to ask him to think about it. I attempted to introduce the topic last night, but he pretended to not hear me. I won't give up, though. I'm going to try to persuade him to go. Our relationship deserves to have a chance, and I'm prepared give it one. But I want John feels the same way. I'm patient, but I can't afford waiting forever.

4 PERSONALIZATION

What do you expect from your friends? Write about yourself. Use infinitives.

1. I expect _____

2. I would like _____

3. I urge _____

4. I try to persuade _____

5. _____

INFINITIVES OF PURPOSE

1 AFFIRMATIVE AND NEGATIVE STATEMENTS

Read the pairs of sentences. Combine them, using the infinitive of purpose.

1. I went to Lacy's department store. I wanted to buy some clothes.

   <u>I went to Lacy's department store to buy some clothes.</u>

2. He bought an alarm clock. He didn't want to oversleep.

   <u>He bought an alarm clock in order not to oversleep.</u>

3. She used her credit card. She didn't want to pay right away.

   _____

4. I asked for the dressing room. I wanted to try on a dress.

   _____

5. They went to the snack bar. They wanted to get a drink.

   _____

6. I'm going to wait for a sale. I want to save some money.

   _____

7. She tried on the blouse. She wanted to be sure of the size.

   _____

8. He only took fifty dollars with him. He didn't want to spend more.

   _____

9. They went to Lacy's on Monday. They didn't want to miss the sale.

   _____

10. I always go shopping early. I want to avoid the crowds.

    _____

2 AFFIRMATIVE AND NEGATIVE STATEMENTS

These conversations take place in a department store. Complete them.
Use the verbs in the box and the infinitive of purpose.

~~ask~~	cut	have	pay	sign
carry	find out	miss	return	waste

1. A: Before we start looking around, I want to go to the information desk.

   B: Oh. Why do you need to go there?

   A: _____To ask_____ where the petites department is. I can never find

   it. They keep changing its location.

2. A: I'd like to return this.

   B: Do you have the receipt?

   A: No, I don't. I got it as a gift, and I really can't use it.

   B: Hmm. I see there's no price tag on it. I'm sorry, but you need the receipt or the

   price tag _____ it.

3. A: Do you always pay by credit card?

   B: Most of the time. What about you?

   A: No. I don't like to pay finance charges. It ends up being more expensive that way.

   B: I know what you mean. I always pay the bill immediately _____

   a finance charge.

4. A: Can I please have a shopping bag?

   B: Sure.

   A: Thanks. I need one _____ all this stuff.

5. A: Do you have a pen?

   B: Here you are.

   A: Thanks. I need one _____ my name.

(continued on next page)

6. **A:** I'm hungry.

   B: Me too. Let's go to the food court _____ a snack.

   A: Good idea. I always get hungry when I go shopping.

7. **A:** Do you have a sharper knife? I need one _____ this

   steak. It's a little tough.

   B: I'm sorry. I'll bring you one right away.

8. **A:** How do those shoes fit?

   B: I'm not sure. They may be a little tight.

   A: Walk around a little _____ if they're the right size.

9. **A:** We should leave now.

   B: Why? It's only 5:00.

   A: I know. But we have to leave now _____ the express bus.

10. **A:** Here's the up escalator, but where's the escalator going down?

    B: Oh, let's just take the elevator _____ time.

---

❸ EDITING

Read this note. Find and correct four mistakes in the use of the
infinitive of purpose. The first mistake is already corrected.

> Eva—
>
>   I went to the store ~~for~~ to get some eggs and other things for dinner.
> I set the alarm on the electronic organizer to remind you to put the
> turkey in the oven. Could you call Cindi too ask her to bring some
> dessert? Tell her she should come straight from school in order to be
> not late. We'll eat at 6:00—if that's OK with you. Remember—you
> can use the Datalator for checking the vegetable casserole recipe. I've
> got to run in order to get back in time to help you!
>
>   M.

INFINITIVES
WITH *TOO* AND *ENOUGH*

1 WORD ORDER

Put the words in the correct order to make sentences about a new job.

1. near / for me / it's / to walk to work / enough

    <u>It's near enough for me to walk to work.</u>   +

2. too / it's / noisy / for me / to concentrate

_____

3. varied / to be interesting / the work / enough / is

_____

4. for me / the salary / enough / to support my family / is / high

_____

5. to hold / my desk / small / is / too / all my things

_____

6. late / I / sleep / enough / can / to feel awake in the morning

_____

7. for me / my boss / quickly / to understand him / speaks / too

_____

8. aren't / low / the bookshelves / to reach / for me / enough

_____

Now look at the sentences you wrote. Put a plus (+) next to all the positive points. Put a minus (–) next to all the negative points.

2 INFINITIVES WITH *TOO* AND *ENOUGH*

Complete these conversations that take place at the workplace.

1. **A:** Can you read the boss's handwriting?

   B: No. It's _____ too messy for me to read _____.
   (messy / me / read)

2. **A:** It's 11:00 A.M. Do you think we can call Mr. Lin in San Francisco?

   B: Sure. It's 8:00 A.M. there. That's _____.
   (late / call)

3. **A:** Could you help me with those boxes?

   B: Sorry. They're _____. I have a bad back.
   (heavy / me / carry)

4. **A:** You're not drinking your coffee! What's the matter with it?

   B: It's _____. It tastes like someone put about four
   (sweet / drink)
   tablespoons of sugar in it.

5. **A:** Do you think we can put the fax machine on that shelf?

   B: Sure. It's _____.
   (small / fit)

6. **A:** Can you keep the noise down, please? It's _____.
   (noisy / me / think)

   B: Sorry. We'll try to be quieter.

7. **A:** Did you hear that Alex is retiring?

   B: You're kidding! He's not even fifty. He's _____.
   (old / retire)

8. **A:** Can you turn on the air conditioner, please?

   B: The air conditioner! It's _____ the air conditioner.
   (hot / need)
   What are you going to do in August when it really gets hot?

9. **A:** You sound really sick. Maybe you should call the doctor.

   B: Oh. I'm _____ the doctor. I just need to get some rest.
   (sick / call)

10. **A:** Can you help me get that box? It's _____.
    (high / me / reach)

    B: Sure.

3 EDITING

*Read this letter home from a boy in Boy Scout camp. Find and correct
seven mistakes in the use of the infinitive with* **too** *and* **enough**. *The
first mistake is already corrected.*

Dear Mom and Dad,

I'm almost ~~to~~ **too** tired to write. I can't believe how hard Boy Scout camp is.

○ Today we went out on a two-hour hike. It was over 90° in the shade! It was
too hot for to think. We had to take a lot of stuff with us, too. My backpack
was too heavy for me to lift it. I don't think I'm too strong to complete the
program. How did I get into this mess? Is it too late too get out?

Please write.

Love,

Andy

○ P.S. The food is terrible. It's not enough good to eat. Can
you send some candy bars?

P.P.S. Here's a photo of me in case it's been to long for
you to remember what I look like!

---

4 PERSONALIZATION

Complete these sentences about your home or classroom.

1. It's too _____

2. It's _____ enough _____

3. It isn't too _____

4. It isn't _____ enough _____

GERUNDS AND INFINITIVES

1 GERUND OR INFINITIVE

Complete this notice about neighborhood crime prevention. Use the correct form of the verbs in parentheses ( ).

Join Your Neighborhood Watch

_____Making_____ our neighborhood safe is our main concern.
1. (make)

Here are some safety tips:

• Remember _____to lock_____ your doors and windows when you go out.
2. (lock)

• Don't forget _____ some lights on when you're not at home.
3. (leave)

• Avoid _____ alone on dark, deserted streets.
4. (walk)

• Learn _____ aware of your surroundings.
5. (be)

• Don't stop _____ for your house keys. Have them in your hand
6. (look)
before you get to the door.

• Consider _____ a class in self-defense. The Adult Center offers
7. (take)
free classes.

• Don't hesitate _____ a police officer for help.
8. (ask)
It's better to be safe than sorry. Stop _____ in
9. (live)
fear. Join your Neighborhood Watch.

The next meeting is at 7:00 P.M. Tuesday, March 3, at the

Community Center.

Please attend! We look forward to _____ you there!
10. (see)

2 GERUND OR INFINITIVE

These conversations took place at a community center. Complete the summary statements about them. Choose the right verbs or expressions from the box and use the gerund or infinitive form of the verbs in parentheses ( ).

afford	be tired of	~~enjoy~~	intend	quit	remember
agree	believe in	forget	offer	refuse	stop

1. **JOE:** Have you ever been to one of these meetings before?

   NANCY: Yes. You get a lot of useful tips. Besides, I like to meet my neighbors.

   Nancy _____<u>enjoys meeting</u>_____ her neighbors.
   (meet)

2. **ANDREA:** Why did you start coming to these meetings?

   FRANK: My apartment was broken into twice. I've had enough. I want to do

   something about it.

   Frank _____ a crime victim.
   (be)

3. **CRAIG:** Would you like a cup of coffee?

   SYLVIE: Oh, no thanks.

   CRAIG: Don't you drink coffee?

   SYLVIE: I used to, but I gave it up a year ago.

   Sylvie _____ coffee.
   (drink)

4. **CARYN:** I think these meetings are really important. You can get a lot accomplished

   when you work with other people.

   FERNANDO: I know what you mean.

   Caryn _____ with other people.
   (work)

5. **JANE:** Did you bring Gerry's book?

   SARA: Oh, no. I left it at work.

   Jane _____ Gerry's book.
   (bring)

6. **SHARON:** Did you lock the windows before we left the house?

   JIM: No, *you* locked the windows. I saw you do it.

   SHARON: That's strange. I don't _____ them!
   (lock)

(continued on next page)

7.   **TOM:** You're late. I was getting worried.

        BETSY: I'm sorry. On the way over here, I noticed that I was almost out of gas. So I

        went to fill up the tank.

Betsy _____ gas.
             (get)

8.   **CATHY:** I really don't like the neighborhood anymore.

        MIKE: So why don't you move?

        CATHY: The rents are too high everywhere else.

Cathy can't _____.
                   (move)

9.   **CAMILLE:** I was afraid to come to the meeting tonight.

        VILMA: Well, I just *won't* live in fear.

Vilma _____ in fear.
               (live)

10.   **SARA:** Do you have a burglar alarm?

        DAVE: No. But I'm definitely going to get one.

Dave _____ a burglar alarm.
            (get)

11.   **RACHEL:** Do you think you could help us organize the next meeting?

        WALTER: OK. When is it scheduled for?

        RACHEL: We don't have a date yet, but I'll let you know.

Walter _____ with the next meeting.
               (help)

12.   **AXEL:** Would you like a ride home?

        JOANNA: Thanks. That would be great.

        AXEL: We'll be leaving in about five minutes.

        JOANNA: I'll be ready.

Axel _____ Joanna home.
            (drive)

③ GERUND OR INFINITIVE

Rewrite these sentences. Use the gerund or infinitive.

1. It's important to know your neighbors.

  Knowing your neighbors is important.

2. Going to the community center is fun.

  It's fun to go to the community center.

3. It's wise to be cautious.

  _____

4. Walking on ice is dangerous.

  _____

5. Installing a burglar alarm is a good idea.

  _____

6. It's not good to be afraid all the time.

  _____

7. Walking alone on a dark, deserted street is risky.

  _____

8. Working together is helpful.

  _____

④ PERSONALIZATION

Write about safety measures you take. Use gerunds and infinitives.

1. I avoid _____

2. I always try _____

3. It's important _____

4. I keep _____

5. I try to remember _____

6. _____

UNIT

32 PREFERENCES: PREFER, WOULD PREFER, WOULD RATHER

1 AFFIRMATIVE STATEMENTS

Alicia ranked the following leisure-time activities according to her preferences. (1 = what Alicia likes most; 10 = what Alicia likes least.)

> **Leisure-Time**
> **Preferences**
>
> _5_ cook
> _3_ watch TV
> _2_ go to the movies
> _1_ read a book
> _10_ play cards
> _9_ go for a walk
> _4_ visit friends
> _7_ talk on the phone
> _6_ eat out
> _8_ listen to music

Write about Alicia's preferences.

1. cook / eat out

   Alicia prefers _____ *cooking to eating out.* _____

2. listen to music / go for a walk

   She'd rather _____

3. read a book / visit friends

   She prefers _____

4. visit friends / talk on the phone

   She prefers _____

5. watch TV / go to the movies

   She'd rather _____

6. talk on the phone / listen to music

She'd rather _____

7. play cards / go to the movies

She prefers _____

8. watch TV / listen to music

She prefers _____

9. read a book / watch TV

She'd rather _____

10. play cards / read a book

She prefers _____

② AFFIRMATIVE AND NEGATIVE STATEMENTS

Ralph is in the hospital. He completed this meal form.

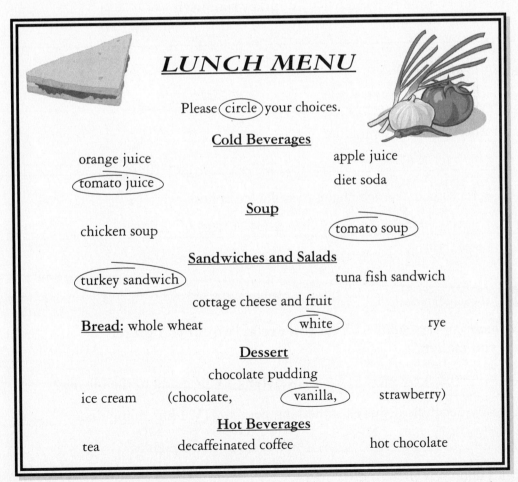

LUNCH MENU

Please (circle) your choices.

Cold Beverages

orange juice   apple juice

(tomato juice)   diet soda

Soup

chicken soup   (tomato soup)

Sandwiches and Salads

(turkey sandwich)   tuna fish sandwich

cottage cheese and fruit

Bread: whole wheat   (white)   rye

Dessert

chocolate pudding

ice cream   (chocolate,   vanilla,   strawberry)

Hot Beverages

tea   decaffeinated coffee   hot chocolate

(continued on next page)

Use the cues to make sentences about Ralph's preferences.

1. He'd rather / diet soda

   He'd rather not have diet soda.

2. He'd prefer / juice

3. He'd rather / apple juice / tomato juice

4. He'd rather / a hot beverage

5. He'd prefer / chicken soup

6. He'd prefer / a sandwich / cottage cheese and fruit

7. He'd prefer / a tuna fish sandwich / a turkey sandwich

8. He'd rather / white bread

9. He'd rather / chocolate pudding

10. He'd prefer / chocolate ice cream / vanilla ice cream

3 QUESTIONS

Complete these conversations with **do you prefer**, **would you prefer**, *or* **would you rather**.

1. A: _____ _Do you prefer_ _____ watching TV or going to the movies?

   B: It really depends. If there's something good on TV, I like doing that.

2. A: _____ newspapers to magazines?

   B: Oh. I definitely prefer newspapers.

3. A: I don't feel like going out.

   B: _____ stay home?

   A: Yes, I think I would.

4. A: I've got vanilla and chocolate ice cream. Which _____

   have?

   B: Chocolate, please.

5. A: I thought we could stay home tonight.

   B: Really?

   A: _____ go out?

   B: Well, there's a good movie at the Quad.

6. A: There's a show at 8:00 and one at 10:00. _____ the early

   or the late show?

   B: Let's go to the early show.

7. A: Could you get me some juice?

   B: Sure. _____ orange or grapefruit?

   A: Orange, please.

8. A: How do you like to spend your free time? _____ doing

   things with friends or doing things alone?

   B: It depends. I need time for my friends, and I need time to be alone.

4 PERSONALIZATION

Look at the menu in Exercise 2. Complete these sentences with true information.

1. I'd prefer _____

2. I'd rather not _____

3. I'd prefer not _____

33 NECESSITY: HAVE (GOT) TO, DON'T HAVE TO, MUST, MUST NOT, CAN'T

1 AFFIRMATIVE AND NEGATIVE STATEMENTS WITH *MUST*

Complete these rules from the California driver's handbook. Use the words in the box with **must** or **must not**.

allow	drink	~~have~~	send	turn on
be	drive	place	stop	wear

1. If you are a resident of California and drive a motor vehicle on a public highway, you _____ must have _____ a California driver's license.

2. You _____ your child under the age of 18 years to drive on a highway without a license or permit.

3. An instruction permit does not allow you to drive alone. An adult who has a driver's license _____ in the car with you.

4. When you move, you _____ your new address to the Department of Motor Vehicles in ten days.

5. You _____ so slowly that you are a danger on the road. You can get a ticket for driving too slowly as well as for driving too fast.

6. The law says adults _____ their children in approved safety seats (if a child is under 4 years old or weighs less than 40 pounds).

7. The law says you _____ your headlights when you drive from 30 minutes after sunset until 30 minutes before sunrise, and any other time when you can see less than 1,000 feet ahead of you.

8. The driver of a vehicle _____ a headset over, or earplugs in, both ears.

9. It is illegal to leave the scene of an accident. You _____ your car.

10. As in all states, driving under the influence of alcohol is against the law in California. You _____ and drive!

❷ AFFIRMATIVE AND NEGATIVE STATEMENTS WITH *HAVE TO*

In the United States, motor vehicle rules differ from state to state. Look at the chart. Complete the statements with **have to** *or* **don't have to** *and the verbs in parentheses ( ).*

	AGE FOR REGULAR LICENSE	DRIVER'S EDUCATION CLASS REQUIRED	LICENSE DURATION	FEE	ANNUAL SAFETY INSPECTION	SEAT BELT LAW
Alaska	16	No	5 yrs.	$15.00	No	Yes
California	18	No	4 yrs.	$12.00	No	Yes
Florida	16	No	4 yrs.	$20.00	No	Yes
Massachusetts	18	Yes	5 yrs.	$33.75	Yes	Yes
New Hampshire	18	No	4 yrs.	$32.50	Yes	No
New York	17	Yes	4 yrs.	$22.25	Yes	Yes
Texas	16	No	4 yrs.	$16.00	Yes	Yes
Washington, D.C.	16	No	4 yrs.	$10.50	Yes	Yes

(continued on next page)

1. You _____have to be_____ 18 to get a California driver's license.
   (be)

2. You _____ 18 to get a license in Alaska.
   (be)

3. You _____ a driver's education class in order to get your
   (take)
   license in Florida.

4. You _____ a driver's education course in New York.
   (complete)

5. In Massachusetts, you _____ your license every four years.
   (renew)

6. In Washington, D.C., you _____ your license every four
   (renew)
   years.

7. You _____ a $33.75 fee for a Massachusetts license.
   (pay)

8. You _____ as much for an Alaska license.
   (pay)

9. You _____ your car for a yearly inspection in New York.
   (take)

10. You _____ a yearly inspection in Florida.
    (get)

11. You _____ a seat belt in Texas.
    (wear)

12. You _____ a seat belt in New Hampshire.
    (wear)

3 CONTRAST: *MUST NOT* OR *DON'T HAVE TO*

Look again at the chart in Exercise 2. Complete these statements with
must not *or* **don't have to**.

1. If you are under the age of 16, you _____must not_____ drive in the state
   of California.

2. You _____ be 18 to drive in the state of Texas.

3. You _____ take a driver's education course in most of the
   states.

4. You _____ renew your license every four years in
   Massachusetts.

5. You _____ drive with an expired license.

6. You _____ pay a $20.00 license fee in Washington, D.C.

7. You _____ have an annual car inspection in Florida.

8. You _____ forget to have your car inspected annually if

you live in Washington, D.C.

9. You _____ drive without a seat belt in Florida.

10. You _____ wear a seat belt in New Hampshire.

4 STATEMENTS, QUESTIONS, AND SHORT ANSWERS WITH *HAVE TO*

Complete these conversations. Use the correct form of **have to** *and the verbs in parentheses ( ). Use short answers when necessary. Be sure to use the correct tense.*

1. A: Did you pass your road test the first time you took it?

   B: No. I _____ had to take _____ it two more times before I passed!
                      (take)

2. A: _____ we _____ for gas?
                           (stop)

   B: _____. The tank's almost empty.

3. A: How many times _____ you _____ public
                             (use)

transportation since you moved to Los Angeles?

   B: Only once. When my car broke down.

4. A: _____ you _____ late yesterday?
                         (work)

   B: _____. Luckily, I finished on time.

5. A: Are you thinking of buying a new car?

   B: Not yet. But in a couple of years I _____ another one.
                         (get)

6. A: Why didn't you come to the meeting last night?

   B: I _____ my uncle to the airport.
          (drive)

7. A: My wife got a speeding ticket last week.

   B: Really? How much _____ she

_____?
     (pay)

   A: It was more than $100.

(continued on next page)

8. A: _____ your son ever _____
(pay)

for a traffic violation?

B: _____. He's a very careful driver.

9. A: _____ you _____ a new
(get)

license when you move?

B: _____. You can only use an out-of-state license for ten

days.

10. A: Do you have car insurance?

B: Of course. Everyone in New York _____ car insurance.
(have)

---

5 **CONTRAST:** *MUST, MUST NOT, HAVE TO, DON'T HAVE TO, AND CAN'T*

Read these test questions about road signs. Write the letter of the correct answer in the box.

---

1. When you see [YIELD] it means:

    a. You must come to a complete stop.
    b. You must not stop.
    c. You don't have to stop, but you must slow down and prepare
       to stop if necessary.

ANS
C

---

2. When you see [STOP] it means:

    a. You don't have to stop.
    b. You must stop.
    c. You can't stop.

ANS

---

3. When you see [SPEED LIMIT 50] it means:

    a. You must drive 50 miles per hour.
    b. You must not drive faster than 50 miles per hour.
    c. You don't have to drive more than 50 miles per hour.

ANS

4. When you see　NO TURN ON RED　it means:

    a. You have to turn when the light is red.

    b. You don't have to turn when the light is red.

    c. You must not turn when the light is red.

ANS ☐

5. When you see　DO NOT ENTER　it means:

    a. You must not enter.

    b. You don't have to enter.

    c. You must enter.

ANS ☐

6. When you see　DO NOT PASS　it means:

    a. You don't have to pass another car.

    b. You can't pass another car.

    c. You have to pass another car.

ANS ☐

7. When you see　ONE WAY ➤　it means:

    a. You must drive in the direction of the arrow.

    b. You must not drive in the direction of the arrow.

    c. You don't have to drive in the direction of the arrow.

ANS ☐

8. When you see　MAXIMUM SPEED 65 / MINIMUM SPEED 45　it means:

    a. You have to drive 45 miles per hour or slower.

    b. You can't drive 70 miles per hour.

    c. You don't have to drive 70 miles per hour.

ANS ☐

6 PERSONALIZATION

Complete these sentences with information about yourself.

1. Next week, I have to _____

2. I don't have to _____

3. I must not _____

4. I can't _____

EXPECTATIONS:
BE SUPPOSED TO

1 AFFIRMATIVE AND NEGATIVE STATEMENTS
WITH *BE SUPPOSED TO*

Today when people get married, the groom's family often shares the expenses, and older couples often pay for their own weddings. However, some people are still traditional. Read the chart and complete the sentences.

Traditional Division of Wedding Expenses

Responsibilities of the Bride's Family	Responsibilities of the Groom's Family
send invitations pay for food supply flowers pay for the groom's ring provide music	pay for the bride's ring give a rehearsal dinner finance the honeymoon

---

1. The groom's parents _____aren't supposed to send_____ the invitations.

2. The bride's family _are supposed to send_ the invitations.

3. The bride's parents _are supposed to provide_ music.

4. The groom's family _aren't supposed to pay for_ the groom's ring.

5. The groom's family _supposed to pay for_ the bride's ring.

6. The bride's parents _aren't supposed to finance_ the honeymoon.

7. The groom's family _are supposed to finance_ the honeymoon.

8. The bride's parents _aren't supposed to give_ the rehearsal dinner.

9. The groom's family _aren't supposed to supply_ the flowers.

10. The bride's family _are supposed to pay_ the food.

❷ AFFIRMATIVE AND NEGATIVE STATEMENTS WITH *BE SUPPOSED TO*

Linda Nelson is getting married. She completed this change of address form, but she made eight mistakes. Find the mistakes and write sentences with **was supposed to** *and* **wasn't supposed to**. *Include the number of the item.*

U.S. Postal Sevice **CHANGE OF ADDRESS ORDER**	Customer Instructions: Complete Items 1 thru 9, Except Item 8, please PRINT all information including address on face of card.	**OFFICIAL USE ONLY**

1. Change of address for *(Check one)* ☑ Individual ☑ Entire Family ☐ Business

Zone/Route Id No.

2. Start Date Month `3 0` Day `0 6` Year `9 5` **3.** If TEMPORARY address, print date to discontinue forwarding Month Day Year

Date Entered on Form 3982 M M D D Y Y

4. Print Last Name or Name of Business *(If more than one use, use separate Change of Address Order Form for each)* `L I N D A`

Expiration Date M M D D Y Y

5. Print First Name of Head of Household (include Jr., Sr., etc.). Leave Blank if the Change of Address Order is for a business. `N e l s o n`

Clerk/Carrier Endorsements

6. Print OLD mailing address, number and street *(if Puerto Rico, include urbanization zone)* `2 6   M A P L E   R O A D`

Apt./Suite No. `4 A` P.O. Box No. R.R/HCR No. Rural Box/HCR Box No.

City `B O S T O N` State `M A` Zip Code `-`

7. Print NEW Mailing address, number and street *(if Puerto Rico, include urbanization zone)* `2 9 8 7   C O S B Y   A V E`

Apt./Suite No. P.O. Box No. R.R/HCR No. Rural Box/HCR Box No.

City `A M H E R S T` State Zip Code `0 1 0 0 2 -`

8. Signature *(See conditions on reverse)* Linda Nelson

OFFICIAL USE ONLY

9. Date Signed Month Day Year

OFFICIAL USE ONLY

Verification Endorsement

PS Form 3575, June 1991 ☆ U.S.G.P.O. 1992-309-315

---

1. Item ___1___ <u>She was supposed to check one box.</u>

OR

<u>She wasn't supposed to check two boxes.</u>

2. Item ___2___ <u>She was supposed to write the month first.</u>

3. Item ___3___ <u>She wasn't supposed to write first name.</u>

4. Item _____

5. Item _____

6. Item _____

7. Item _____

8. Item _____

3 QUESTIONS AND ANSWERS WITH *BE SUPPOSED TO*

Linda and her new husband are on their honeymoon. Complete the
conversations. Use the words in the box and **be supposed to**. *Use*
short answers when necessary.

~~arrive~~	call	get	leave	shake
be	do	land	rain	tip

1. **LINDA:** What time _____are_____ we _____supposed to arrive_____ in Bermuda?

   FRANK: Well, the plane _____ at 10:30, but it looks like we're

   going to be late.

2. **LINDA:** What time _____ we _____ to the hotel?

   FRANK: Check-in time is 12:00.

3. **LINDA:** _____ we _____ if we're going to be late?

   FRANK: _____. We'd better look for a phone as soon as we

   land.

4. **FRANK:** How much _____ we _____ the person

   who carries our bags?

   LINDA: I think it's $1.00 a bag.

5. **FRANK:** _____ the hotel restaurant _____ good?

   LINDA: _____. The travel agent suggested that we go

   somewhere else for dinner.

6. **LINDA:** What _____ we _____ with our keys when

   we leave the hotel?

   FRANK: We _____ them at the front desk.

7. **LINDA:** _____ it _____ today?

   FRANK: _____. But look at those clouds. I think we'd better

   take an umbrella just in case.

8. **LINDA:** Can you hand me that bottle of sunblock?

   FRANK: Sure. _____ you _____ the bottle before

   you use it?

   LINDA: I don't know. What do the instructions say?

FUTURE POSSIBILITY:
MAY, MIGHT, COULD

 AFFIRMATIVE AND NEGATIVE STATEMENTS

Use the cues to complete this journal entry.

Thursday, July 3

I was supposed to go to the beach tomorrow, but they say it

_____ might rain _____. I don't know what I'll do. I
　　　　1. (might / rain)

_____ shopping at the mall, instead. It's a
　　　2. (may / go)

holiday weekend, so there _____ some good sales.
　　　　　　　　3. (could / be)

Maybe I'll call Julie. She _____ to go with me.
　　　　　　　4. (might / want)

On second thought, she _____ home. She often
　　　　　　　5. (may / be)

goes away on holiday weekends. I don't know. Shopping

_____ such a good idea. The stores will probably
　　　6. (might / be)

be really crowded. I _____ to a movie. There's a
　　　　　　　7. (could / go)

Spanish movie at Cinema 8. I'm not sure. I'm afraid I

_____ enough of it. My Spanish really isn't that
　　8. (might / understand)

good. Maybe I'll call Ed and ask him if he wants to take a drive to see Aunt

Marla and Uncle Phil. He _____ go. He
　　　　　　　　9. (might / want to)

doesn't like driving in the rain. Oh well, I _____
　　　　　　　　　　　10. (could / stay)

home and read a good book.

---

2 CONTRAST: *BE GOING TO* OR *MIGHT*

Read these conversations. Complete the summary sentences with **be going to** *or* **might** *and the verbs in the box.*

buy	go	rain	see	work
call	have	read	~~visit~~	write

1. **LINDA:** Hello, Julie? This is Linda. Do you want to go to the mall with me?

   JULIE: I don't know. I'm thinking about going to my parents'. I'm not sure. Can I call

   you back?

   Julie _____ *might visit* _____ her parents.

2. **JULIE:** What are you looking for at the mall?

   LINDA: I need to get a new suit for work. I hope I can find one.

   Linda _____ a suit.

3. **LINDA:** Do you think we'll get some rain?

   CARL: Definitely. Look at those clouds.

   Carl thinks it _____.

4. **LINDA:** What are you doing today?

   CARL: I have tickets for a play.

   Carl _____ a play.

5. **LINDA:** What are you doing this weekend?

   SUE: I'm not sure. I'm thinking about taking a drive to the country. It depends on

   the weather.

   Sue _____ for a ride.

6. **LINDA:** Say, Ed. Do you want to see Aunt Marla and Uncle Phil tomorrow?

   ED: I can't. I have to go into the office this weekend.

   Ed _____ this weekend.

7. **LINDA:** How about dinner Saturday night?

   ED: That's an idea. Can I call and let you know tomorrow?

   Linda and Ed _____ dinner together.

8. **LINDA:** Hi, Aunt Marla. How are you?

   MARLA: Linda! How are you? It's good to hear your voice. Listen, we just started

   dinner. Can I call you back?

   LINDA: Sure.

   MARLA: OK. I'll speak to you soon.

   Marla _____ Linda.

9. **MARLA:** This is Aunt Marla. Sorry about before. What are you doing home on a

   holiday weekend?

   LINDA: I'm tired. I just want to stay home with a good book.

   Linda _____ a book.

10. **MARLA:** Do you have any other plans?

   LINDA: Maybe I'll catch up on some of my correspondence.

   Linda _____ some letters.

3 EDITING

Read Linda's letter. Find and correct four mistakes in the use of modals to express future possibility. The first mistake is already corrected.

> Dear Roberta,
>
> How are you? It's the Fourth of July, and it's raining really hard. They say it
> might OR may
> could clear up later. Then again, it ~~could~~ not. You never know with the weather.
>
> Do you remember my brother, Ed? He says hi. He might has dinner with me on
> Saturday night. We may go to a new Mexican restaurant that opened in the mall.
>
> I definitely might take some vacation next month. Perhaps we could do something
> together. It might not be fun to do some traveling. What do you think? Let me
> know.
>
> Love,
>
> Linda

4 **PERSONALIZATION**

Make a short "To Do" list for next weekend. Put a question mark (?)
next to the things you aren't sure you'll do.

To Do

1.

2.

3.

4.

5.

6.

7.

8.

Now write sentences about what you **are going to do** *and what you*
might do.

1. _____

2. _____

3. _____

4. _____

5. _____

6. _____

7. _____

8. _____

ASSUMPTIONS: MUST, HAVE (GOT) TO, MAY, MIGHT, COULD, CAN'T

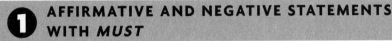

❶ AFFIRMATIVE AND NEGATIVE STATEMENTS WITH *MUST*

Read the facts. Complete the conclusions with **must** *or* **must not***.*

1. Jack is wearing a gold wedding band on his ring finger.

He _____*must be*_____ married.

    (be)

2. You have been calling Alicia since 8:00 P.M., but no one answers the phone.

She _____ at home.

    (be)

3. Jackie got 98 percent on her math test.

Her parents _____ proud of her.

    (feel)

4. Carlos works from 9:00 to 5:00 and then attends night school.

He _____ a lot of free time.

    (have)

5. Martin works as a mechanic in Al's Automobile Shop.

He _____ a lot about cars.

    (know)

6. Monica owns two houses and four cars.

She _____ a lot of money.

    (have)

7. Mr. Cantor always asks me to repeat what I say.

He _____ well.

    (hear)

8. Chen only got four hours of sleep last night.

He _____ very tired today.

    (feel)

153

(continued on next page)

9. Carmen was born in Mexico and moved to the United States when she was ten.

She _____ Spanish.
(speak)

10. Mindy never gets good grades.

She _____ enough.
(study)

11. Dan just bought a bottle of aspirin and four boxes of tissues.

He _____ a cold.
(have)

12. Ana and Giorgio didn't have any of the steak.

They _____ meat.
(eat)

2 CONTRAST: *MUST* OR *MAY / MIGHT / COULD*

Circle the correct words to complete these conversations.

1. A: Someone broke into the Petersons' house.

B: That's terrible! What did they take?

A: All of Mrs. Peterson's jewelry.

B: Oh, no. She could / must feel awful.

2. A: Is she home now?

B: I don't know. She might / must be home. She sometimes gets home by 6:00.

3. A: Do the Petersons have insurance?

B: Oh, they could / must. Mr. Peterson works at an insurance company.

4. A: Have you checked our burglar alarm lately?

B: Yes. And I just put in a new battery.

A: Good. So it must / might be OK.

5. A: Do you remember that guy we saw outside the Petersons' home last week?

B: Yes. Why? Do you think he might / must be the burglar?

6. A: I don't know. I guess he must / could be the burglar. He looked a little suspicious.

B: Maybe we should tell the police about him.

7. A: Someone's at the door.

B: Who <u>could / must</u> it be?

A: I don't know.

8. A: Detective Kramer wanted to ask us some questions about the burglary.

B: Oh. It <u>must / could</u> be him. We're not expecting anybody else.

9. A: How old do you think Detective Kramer is?

B: Well, he's been a detective for ten years. So he <u>must / might</u> be at least thirty-five.

10. A: You're right. He <u>couldn't / might not</u> be much younger than thirty-five. He probably started out as a police officer and became a detective in his early twenties.

B: He looks a lot younger, though.

③ SHORT ANSWERS WITH *MUST* OR *MAY / MIGHT / COULD*

Answer the questions. Include **be** *when necessary.*

1. A: Is Ron a detective?

B: _____ He might be _____. He always carries a notepad.

2. A: Does Marta speak Spanish?

B: _____. She lived in Spain for four years.

3. A: Do the Taylors have a lot of money?

B: _____. They have two homes, and they're always taking expensive vacations.

4. A: Is Ricardo married?

B: _____. He wears a wedding ring.

5. A: Does Anna know Meng?

B: _____. They both work for the same company, but there are more than 100 employees.

6. A: Is your phone out of order?

B: _____. It hasn't rung once today, and John always calls me by this time.

(continued on next page)

7. A: Are Marcia and Scott married?

    B: _____. They both have the same last name, but it's

    possible that they're brother and sister.

8. A: Does Glenda drive?

    B: _____. She owns a car.

9. A: Is Oscar an only child?

    B: _____. He's never mentioned a brother or sister. I really

    don't know.

10. A: Are the Hendersons away?

    B: _____. I haven't seen them for a week, and there are no

    lights on in their apartment.

4 **CONTRAST:** *MUST, COULD, CAN'T, COULDN'T, MIGHT NOT*

Read the description of a burglary suspect and look at the four pictures.
Complete the conversation with the correct words and the names of the
men in the pictures.

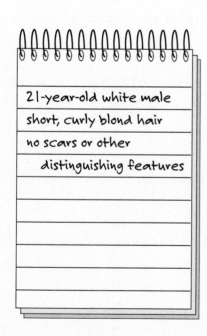

21-year-old white male
short, curly blond hair
no scars or other
   distinguishing features

Allen

Bob

Chet

Dave

DETECTIVE: Look at these four photos. It's possible that one of them

_____ could _____ be the man we're looking for. Take your time.
1. (must / could)

WITNESS 1: Hhmm. What do you think? _____ it be this man?
2. (Could / Must)

WITNESS 2: It _____ be _____. He
3. (can't / must)   4. (Name)

has a scar on his face. What about _____? He has
5. (Name)

short blond hair and looks twenty-one.

WITNESS 1: I'm not sure. It _____ be. But it
6. (could / must)

_____ also be _____. He
7. (might / must)   8. (Name)

also has blond hair and looks twenty-one.

WITNESS 2: But he has long hair.

WITNESS 1: The photo _____ be old. Maybe he cut it.
9. (could / couldn't)

WITNESS 2: That's true. Well, it definitely _____ be
10. (couldn't / might not)

_____. He's too old. Maybe we could look at some
11. (Name)

more photos.

⑤ PERSONALIZATION

Read the description of the burglar in Exercise 4. Look at these pictures.
Is one of them the burglar? What's your opinion? Complete the
sentences.

| Ed | Frank | George |

1. It could be _____ because _____.

2. It couldn't be _____ because _____.

3. It might be _____ because _____.

6 EDITING

Read this woman's journal entry. Find and correct six mistakes in the use of modals to express assumptions. The first mistake is already corrected.

> Just got home. It's really cold outside. The temperature ~~could~~ **must** be
>
> below freezing because the walkway is all covered with ice. What a
>
> day! We went down to the police station to look at photos. They must
>
> having hundreds of photos. They kept showing us more and more. We
>
> kept looking, but it was difficult to be sure. After all, we only saw the
>
> burglar for a few seconds. They've gotta have other witnesses besides
>
> us! There were a lot of people at the mall that day. We may not be the
>
> only ones who got a look at the burglar! That's the one thing I'm
>
> certain of! In spite of our uncertainty with the photos, the detective
>
> was very patient. I guess he must be used to witnesses like us.
>
> Nevertheless, it have to be frustrating for him. I know the police may
>
> really want to catch this guy.

NOUNS AND QUANTIFIERS

① KINDS OF NOUNS

Put these nouns into the correct category.

biology	chair	class	country	day	dollar
Election Day	furniture	hamburger	honesty	ink	Japanese
money	news	pen	president	rice	Richard
snow	snowflake	spaghetti	story	sugar	swimming
Yeltsin	zoo				

Proper Nouns

_____   _____

_____   _____

Common Nouns

Count	Non-Count
_____	*biology*
_____	_____
_____	_____
_____	_____
_____	_____
_____	_____
_____	_____
_____	_____
_____	_____
_____	_____

❷ COUNT AND NON-COUNT NOUNS

Complete these food facts. Use the correct form of the words in parentheses ( ).

1. ___Chocolate___ ___has___ a chemical that creates a feeling similar to being in
   (Chocolate)   (have)
   love.

2. _____ _____ the most popular food in the United States.
   (Potato)   (be)
   _____ _____ the most popular food in the world.
   (Rice)   (be)

3. _____ _____ Americans' favorite snack food.
   (Potato chip)   (be)

4. _____ _____ more potato chips than any other _____
   (American)   (eat)   (people)
   in the world.

5. Chewing raw onions for five minutes _____ all the germs in your mouth.
                                        (kill)

6. _____ _____ at least 5,000 years old.
   (Popcorn)   (be)

7. _____ _____ really nuts. They are members of the bean family.
   (Peanut)   (not be)

8. _____ _____ been around for just a little over a hundred years.
   (Peanut butter) (have)
   It's a relatively new health-food invention.

9. The _____ of the hot dog _____ very long. It began 3,500 years
       (history)   (be)
   ago.

10. _____ _____ the favorite dessert in the United States.
    (Ice cream)   (be)

❸ MUCH OR MANY

*Complete this food quiz. Use **much** or **many**. Then try to guess the answer to the questions. Circle the letter of your choice.*

1. How ___much___ Vitamin C does an onion have? As ___much___ as

   ⓐ two apples

   b. one orange

   c. three carrots

2. How _____ rolls are there in a "baker's dozen"?

   a. eleven

   b. twelve

   c. thirteen

3. How _____ pizza does the average person from the United States eat each

  year?

   a. 13 pounds

   b. 23 pounds

   c. 33 pounds

4. In how _____ countries can you find a McDonalds' fast-food restaurant?

   a. almost 50

   b. almost 80

   c. almost 120

5. How _____ chocolate does the average person in Switzerland eat each year?

   a. 10.7 pounds

   b. 20.7 pounds

   c. 30.7 pounds

6. How _____ calories are there in a cup of regular vanilla ice cream?

   a. 170

   b. 270

   c. 370

7. How _____ ice cream does the average person in Finland eat each year?

   a. 22 pints

   b. 38 pints

   c. 46 pints

8. How _____ weeks is it safe to keep butter in the refrigerator?

   a. four

   b. six

   c. eight

4 QUANTIFIERS

Circle the correct words to complete the conversation.

A: How was the party?

B: It was good. I saw (a lot of)/ much people from my childhood.
    1.

A: That's nice. Were there <u>many / much</u> family members there too?
    2.

B: No. Unfortunately <u>a few / few</u> relatives live nearby, so not <u>many / much</u> could come.
    3.   **4.**

A: How was the food?

B: Delicious! In fact, there's so <u>many / much</u> left over, you should come by tonight. I can
    5.

show you the photos too. <u>Several / A great deal of</u> people had cameras with them, and
    6.

we got <u>some / a little</u> pictures back already.
    7.

A: That was fast!

B: Yeah. We brought them to one of those places where you only have to wait <u>a few / few</u>
    8.

hours to get them back.

A: Great! What time should I come over?

B: Let's see. I get out of school at 5:00, and I don't think I'll have <u>a little / much</u> homework
    9.

tonight. How about 7:00?

A: Will that give you <u>enough / many</u> time to get ready?
    10.

B: Sure. There's really nothing to do.

A: OK. See you then.

5 PERSONALIZATION

Describe a party or another social event you've attended. Who was there? What kind of food was served at the event?

_____

_____

_____

_____

_____

Articles: Indefinite and Definite

1 INDEFINITE AND DEFINITE ARTICLES

Circle the correct choice to complete these conversations that take place in school. If you don't need an article, circle Ø.

1. **A:** Can I borrow <u>a</u> / the pen?

   B: Sure. Take <u>a</u> / the one on <u>a</u> / the desk. I don't need it.

2. **A:** Is <u>a</u> / the teacher here yet?

   B: No, she hasn't come yet.

3. **A:** What do you think of Mr. Mencz?

   B: He's <u>a</u> / the best teacher I've ever had.

4. **A:** Have you done <u>the</u> / Ø homework?

   B: Yes. But I don't think I got <u>a</u> / the last answer right.

5. **A:** Could you open <u>a</u> / the window, please?

   B: Which one?

   A: <u>A</u> / The one next to <u>a</u> / the door.

   B: Sure.

6. **A:** Who's that?

   B: That's <u>a</u> / the school principal.

   A: Oh, I've never seen her before.

7. **A:** Do you like <u>the</u> / Ø history?

   B: It's OK. But I prefer <u>the</u> / Ø science.

8. **A:** We learned about <u>an</u> / the ozone layer in science class yesterday.

   B: Did you know there's <u>a</u> / the hole in it?

   A: Yeah. It's pretty scary.

(continued on next page)

9. **A:** What kind of work do you do?

   B: I'm <u>an / the</u> engineer. What about you?

   A: I'm <u>a / Ø</u> mechanic.

10. **A:** Are they <u>some / Ø</u> students?

    B: I don't think so. They look like <u>the / Ø</u> teachers.

11. **A:** Do you know where I can get <u>some / the</u> water around here?

    B: Sure. There's <u>a / the</u> water fountain right across <u>a / the</u> hall, right next to <u>the / Ø</u> rest rooms.

12. **A:** Do you know what <u>a / the</u> homework is for tomorrow?

    B: We have to read <u>a / the</u> fable.

    A: Which one?

    B: <u>A / The</u> one on page 23.

❷ INDEFINITE AND DEFINITE ARTICLES

Complete the conversation. Use **a / an** *or* **the** *when necessary.*

BING YANG: Hi, Georgina. What are you doing?

GEORGINA: I'm reading _____*a*_____ fable for my English class.
1.

BING YANG: What's _____ fable? I've never heard the word before.
2.

GEORGINA: _____ fable is _____ short story about _____
3.   4.   5.
animals.

BING YANG: About _____ animals? Like _____ science story?
6.   7.

GEORGINA: No. It's _____ fiction. _____ animals act like
8.   9.
_____ people. They usually teach _____ lesson.
10.   11.
_____ lesson is called _____ moral of _____
12.   13.   14.
story, and it always comes at _____ end.
15.

BING YANG: That's interesting. Who's _____ author of _____ fable
16.   17.
you're reading?

GEORGINA: Aesop. He was _____ ancient Greek writer.
18.

BING YANG: Oh, now I know what you're talking about. My parents used to read

_____ fables to me when I was _____ child.
              19.   **20.**

GEORGINA: Well, they're also good for _____ adults. I'll lend you
                                          21.

_____ book when I'm finished if you're interested.
22.

BING YANG: Thanks. I am.

3 INDEFINITE AND DEFINITE ARTICLES

Complete this version of an Aesop's fable. Use **a / an** *or* **the** *when necessary.*

The Fox and the Goat

_____A_____ fox fell into _____ well and couldn't get out again. Finally,
     1.   **2.**

_____ thirsty goat came by and saw _____ fox in _____
3.   **4.**   **5.**

well. "Is _____ water good?" _____ goat asked. "Good?" said
          6.   **7.**

_____ fox. "It's _____ best water I've ever tasted in my whole life.
8.   **9.**

Why don't you come down and try it?"

_____ goat was very thirsty, so he jumped into _____ well. When
10.   **11.**

he was finished drinking, he looked for _____ way to get out of
                                         12.

_____ well, but, of course, there wasn't any. Then _____ fox said, "I
13.   **14.**

have _____ excellent idea. Stand on your back legs and place your front legs
     15.

firmly against _____ front side of _____ well. Then, I'll climb onto
               16.   **17.**

(continued on next page)

your back and, from there, I'll step on your horns and be able to get out. When I'm out, I'll

help you get out, too." _____ goat thought this was _____ good idea
18. 19.

and followed _____ advice.
20.

When _____ fox was out of _____ well, he quickly and quietly
21. 22.

walked away. _____ goat called loudly after him and reminded him of
23.

_____ promise he had made to help him out. But _____ fox turned
24. 25.

and said, "You should have as much sense in your head as you have _____
26.

hairs in your beard. You jumped into _____ well before making sure you
27.

could get out again."

Moral: Look before you leap.

ANSWER KEY

Where the full form is given, the contraction is also acceptable. Where the contracted form is given, the full form is also acceptable.

PART ADJECTIVES AND ADVERBS: REVIEW AND EXPANSION

UNIT 22 ADJECTIVES AND ADVERBS

1

2. nice
3. fast
4. well
5. dangerous
6. beautifully
7. hard
8. safely
9. occasional
10. happy
11. sudden
12. carefully
13. angrily
14. unfortunate

2

2. Good news travels fast!
3. It has five large rooms,
4. it's in a very large building.
5. It's not too bad.
6. It seems pretty quiet.
7. the landlord speaks very loudly.
8. He doesn't hear well.
9. Was it a hard decision?
10. we had to decide quickly.
11. I have to leave now.
12. Good luck with your new apartment!

3

2. hard
3. well
4. nice
5. extremely
6. comfortable
7. cold
8. pretty
9. friendly
10. safe
11. really
12. important
13. late
14. completely
15. empty
16. good
17. easily
18. near
19. frequently
20. wonderful

4

2. disturbed
3. entertaining
4. disgusted
5. inspiring
6. paralyzed
7. moving
8. moved
9. frightening
10. disturbed
11. touching
12. astonishing
13. frightening
14. bored
15. disappointed
16. touching
17. exciting
18. entertaining
19. bored

UNIT 23 ADJECTIVES: COMPARATIVES AND EQUATIVES

1

2. more expensive
3. hotter
4. bigger
5. better
6. more difficult
7. prettier
8. more beautiful
9. worse
10. longer
11. farther
12. more careful
13. more dangerous
14. earlier
15. more terrible
16. wider
17. noisier
18. more comfortable
19. wetter
20. cheaper

2

2. larger
3. slower
4. bigger than
5. more quiet / quieter
6. more expensive
7. cheaper than
8. better
9. more convenient
10. farther
11. faster than
12. more comfortable
13. later than
14. settled

3

2. Y . . . cheaper than . . . X.
3. Y . . . larger than . . . X.
4. Y . . . heavier than . . . X.
5. X . . . more efficient than . . . Y.
6. Y . . . more effective than . . . X.
7. Y . . . faster than . . . X.
8. X . . . noisier than . . . Y.
9. Y . . . better than . . . X.
10. X . . . worse than . . . Y.

4

2. not as crowded as
3. not as big as
4. not as cold as
5. as hot as
6. not as wet as
7. not as windy as
8. not as sunny as

5

2. The smaller the city, the lower the crime rate.
3. The warmer the climate, the busier the police.
4. The colder the weather, the greater the number of robberies.
5. The larger the police force, the more violent the city.
6. The later in the day, the higher the number of car thefts.
7. The higher the unemployment rate, the higher the crime rate.
8. The more mobile the population, the more dangerous the city.
9. The more organized the community, the safer the neighborhood.

6

2. is getting less and less crowded.
3. is getting lower and lower.
4. is getting higher and higher.
5. are getting more and more expensive.

7

(Answers will vary.)

UNIT **ADJECTIVES: SUPERLATIVES**

1

2. the funniest
3. the biggest
4. the most wonderful
5. the best
6. the worst
7. the happiest
8. the most important
9. the warmest
10. the most interesting
11. the farthest
12. the most intelligent
13. the slowest
14. the most expensive

2

2. The least expensive
3. Funji
4. the most expensive
5. Minon
6. the lowest
7. Minon
8. the smallest
9. the lightest
10. the most powerful
11. the heaviest
12. Minon
13. the most convenient
14. Rikon
15. the least important

3

2. the smallest
3. the deepest
4. the tallest
5. the longest
6. the farthest
7. the busiest
8. the most popular
9. the most expensive
10. the fastest
11. the slowest
12. the heaviest

UNIT 25 ADVERBS: EQUATIVES, COMPARATIVES, SUPERLATIVES

1

2. faster — the fastest
3. more beautifully — the most beautifully
4. sooner — the soonest
5. more dangerously — the most dangerously
6. better — the best
7. earlier — the earliest
8. more carefully — the most carefully
9. worse — the worst
10. farther — the farthest

2

2. harder than
3. more slowly than OR slower than
4. faster
5. more accurately
6. more aggressively than
7. worse than
8. better
9. more successfully
10. more seriously
11. more regularly than

Winning Team Members: George, Bob, Randy, Dennis
Losing Team Members: Alex, Rick, Larry, Elvin

3

2. ran as fast as
3. jumped as high as
4. didn't jump as high as
5. didn't throw the discus as far as
6. threw the discus as far as
7. didn't do as well as
8. didn't compete as successfully as

❹

2. E . . . the slowest OR the most slowly . . .
   slower OR more slowly than
3. higher than . . . B
4. E . . . the highest
5. farther than . . . E
6. E . . . the farthest
7. E . . . the best

❺

2. She's running more and more frequently.
3. He's throwing the ball farther and farther.
4. She's shooting more and more accurately.
5. He's jumping higher and higher.
6. He's running slower and slower OR more and more slowly.
7. They're skating more and more gracefully.

8. They're practicing harder and harder.
9. He's driving more and more dangerously.

❻

I just completed my run. I'm running much
longer ~~that~~ **than** before. Today I ran for thirty minutes
without getting out of breath. I'm glad I decided
more slowly OR slower
to run ~~more slow~~. The more slowly I run, the
farther
~~farthest~~ I can go. I'm really seeing progress.

Because I'm enjoying it, I run more and more
frequently
~~frequent~~. And the more often I do it, the longer

and farther I can go. I really believe that running

lets me feel better more **quickly** ~~quick~~ than other forms of

exercise. I'm even sleeping better than before!

I'm thinking about running in the next
as fast as OR faster than
marathon. I may not run ~~as fast than~~ younger
longer
runners, but I think I can run ~~long~~ and farther.

We'll see!

PART Ⅵ GERUNDS AND INFINITIVES

UNIT 26 GERUNDS: SUBJECT AND OBJECT

❶

2. going
3. meeting
4. Sitting
5. running
6. lifting
7. doing
8. taking
9. Exercising
10. wasting

❷

2. lifting weights
3. playing tennis
4. dancing
5. Doing sit-ups
6. lifting weights
7. Dancing
8. Walking
9. dancing
10. jogging
11. doing sit-ups OR playing tennis OR jogging
12. doing sit-ups OR playing tennis OR jogging

❸

2. dislikes doing
3. enjoys dancing
4. mind teaching
5. kept practicing
6. denied OR denies stepping
7. considering taking
8. regrets not beginning
9. suggests going
10. admits feeling

❹

(Answers will vary.)

UNIT 27 GERUNDS AFTER PREPOSITIONS

❶

2. of
3. to
4. on
5. in
6. for OR to
7. of
8. in
9. about
10. to

❷

2. succeeded in collecting
3. is worried about missing
4. are used to working
5. believe in talking
6. are tired of waiting
7. insists on reaching
8. approves of having
9. are opposed to going
10. looking forward to returning

❸

2. striking
3. firing
4. permitting
5. being
6. getting
7. missing
8. trying
9. making
10. hearing

④

(Answers will vary.)

UNIT **INFINITIVES AFTER CERTAIN VERBS**

①

2. want to see
3. refuses to go
4. threatened to end
5. hesitate OR am hesitating to take
6. seems to be
7. attempted to create
8. intend to stay
9. needs to speak
10. will agree to go

②

2. to do the dishes, him to do the dishes.
3. her to buy some milk, to buy some milk.
4. him to drive her to her aunt's, to drive her to her aunt's.
5. him to have dinner at her place, to have dinner at her place.
6. him to give her his answer, to give her his answer.
7. to cut his hair, her to cut his hair.
8. him to be home at 7:00, to be home at 8:00.
9. her to call him before she leaves the office, to call him before she left the office.

③

Gabby answered my letter! She advised ~~me~~ us to go to counseling separately. I don't know if John will agree ~~going~~ to go, but I'm going to ask him to think about it. I attempted to introduce the topic last night, but he pretended ~~to not~~ not to hear me. I won't give up, though. I'm going to try to persuade him to go. Our relationship deserves to have a chance, and I'm prepared ∧to give it one. But I want John ~~feels~~ to feel the same way. I'm patient, but I can't afford ~~waiting~~ to wait forever.

④

(Answers will vary.)

UNIT **INFINITIVES OF PURPOSE**

①

3. She used her credit card in order not to pay right away.
4. I asked for the dressing room (in order) to try on a dress.
5. They went to the snack bar (in order) to get a drink.
6. I'm going to wait for a sale (in order) to save some money.
7. She tried on the blouse (in order) to be sure of the size.
8. He only took fifty dollars with him in order not to spend more.
9. They went to Lacy's on Monday in order not to miss the sale.
10. I always go shopping early (in order) to avoid the crowds.

②

2. (in order) to return
3. in order not to pay
4. (in order) to carry
5. (in order) to sign
6. to have
7. (in order) to cut
8. (in order) to find out
9. in order not to miss
10. in order not to waste

③

I went to the store ~~for~~ to get some eggs and other things for dinner. I set the alarm on the electronic organizer to remind you to put the turkey in the oven. Could you call Cindi ~~too~~ to ask her to bring some dessert? Tell her she should come straight from school in order ~~to be not~~ not to be late. We'll eat at 6:00—if that's OK with you. Remember—you can use the Datalator ~~for checking~~ to check the vegetable casserole recipe. I've got to run in order to get back in time to help you!

UNIT **INFINITIVES WITH TOO AND ENOUGH**

①

2. It's too noisy for me to concentrate.
3. The work is varied enough to be interesting.

4. The salary is high enough for me to support my family.
5. My desk is too small to hold all my things.
6. I can sleep late enough to feel awake in the morning.
7. My boss speaks too quickly for me to understand him.
8. The bookshelves aren't low enough for me to reach.

Positive points: 1,3,4,6,9
Negative points: 2,5,7,8,10

2. late enough to call
3. too heavy for me to carry
4. too sweet to drink

5. small enough to fit
6. too noisy for me to think
7. not old enough to retire
8. not hot enough to need
9. not sick enough to call
10. too high for me to reach

I'm almost **too** ~~to~~ tired to write. I can't believe how hard Boy Scout camp is. Today we went out on a two-hour hike. It was over 90° in the shade! It was too hot **to think** OR **for me to think** ~~for to think~~. We had to take a lot of stuff with us, too. My backpack was too heavy for me to lift ~~it~~. I don't think I'm **strong enough** ~~too strong~~ to complete the program. How did I get into this mess? Is it too late **to** ~~to~~ get out? Please write.

P.S. The food is terrible. It's not **good enough** ~~enough good~~ to eat. Can you send some candy bars?

P.P.S. Here's a photo of me in case it's been **too** ~~to~~ long for you to remember what I look like!

(Answers will vary.)

UNIT 31 GERUNDS AND INFINITIVES

3. to leave   7. taking
4. walking   8. to ask
5. to be   9. living
6. to look   10. seeing

2. is tired of being   8. afford to move
3. quit drinking   9. refuses to live
4. believes in working   10. intends to get
5. forgot to bring   11. agreed to help
6. remember locking   12. offered to drive
7. stopped to get

3. Being cautious is wise.
4. It's dangerous to walk on ice.
5. It's a good idea to install a burglar alarm.
6. Being afraid all the time isn't good.
7. It's risky to walk alone on a dark, deserted street.
8. It's helpful to work together.

(Answers will vary.)

PART VII MORE MODALS AND RELATED VERBS AND EXPRESSIONS

UNIT 32 PREFERENCES: PREFER, WOULD PREFER, WOULD RATHER

2. listen to music than go for a walk.
3. reading a book to visiting friends.
4. visiting friends to talking on the phone.
5. go to the movies than watch TV.
6. talk on the phone than listen to music.
7. going to the movies to playing cards.
8. watching TV to listening to music.
9. read a book than watch TV.
10. reading a book to playing cards.

2. He'd prefer (to have) juice.
3. He'd rather have tomato juice than apple juice.
4. He'd rather not have a hot beverage.
5. He'd prefer not to have chicken soup.
6. He'd prefer a sandwich to cottage cheese and fruit.
7. He'd prefer a turkey sandwich to a tuna fish sandwich.
8. He'd rather have white bread.
9. He'd rather not have chocolate pudding.

10. He'd prefer vanilla ice cream to chocolate ice cream.

③

2. Do you prefer
3. Would you rather
4. would you rather
5. Would you rather
6. Would you prefer
7. Would you prefer
8. Do you prefer

④

(Answers will vary.)

UNIT NECESSITY:
HAVE (GOT) TO, DON'T HAVE TO, MUST, MUST NOT, CAN'T,

①

2. must not allow
3. must be
4. must send
5. must not drive
6. must place
7. must turn on
8. must not wear
9. must stop
10. must not drink

②

2. don't have to be
3. don't have to take
4. have to complete
5. don't have to renew
6. have to renew
7. have to pay
8. don't have to pay
9. have to take
10. don't have to get
11. have to wear
12. don't have to wear

③

2. don't have to
3. don't have to
4. don't have to
5. must not
6. don't have to
7. don't have to
8. must not
9. must not
10. don't have to

④

2. **A:** Do . . . have to stop
   B: Yes, we do
3. **A:** have . . . had to use
4. **A:** Did . . . have to work
   B: No, I didn't
5. **B:** 'll have to get OR 'm going to have to get
6. **B:** had to drive
7. **B:** did . . . have to pay
8. **A:** Has . . . had to pay
   B: No, he hasn't
9. **A:** Will OR Do . . . have to get OR Are . . . going to have to get
   B: Yes, I will OR do OR am
10. **B:** has to have

⑤

2. b.
3. b.
4. c.
5. a.
6. b.
7. a.
8. b.

⑥

(Answers will vary.)

UNIT EXPECTATIONS:
BE SUPPOSED TO

①

2. is supposed to send
3. are supposed to provide
4. isn't supposed to pay for
5. is supposed to pay for
6. aren't supposed to finance
7. is supposed to finance
8. aren't supposed to give
9. isn't supposed to supply
10. is supposed to pay for

②

2. Item 2. She was supposed to write the month first. OR She wasn't supposed to write the day first.
3. Item 4. She was supposed to print OR write her last name. OR She wasn't supposed to print OR write her first name.
4. Item 5. She was supposed to print OR write her first name. OR She wasn't supposed to print OR write her last name.
5. Item 6. She was supposed to write OR include her zip code.
6. Item 7. She was supposed to write her state.
7. Item 8. She was supposed to sign her name. OR She wasn't supposed to print her name.
8. Item 9. She was supposed to write the date.

③

1. **F:** is OR was supposed to land
2. **L:** are . . . supposed to get
3. **L:** Are . . . supposed to call; **F:** Yes, we are
4. **F:** are . . . supposed to tip
5. **F:** Is . . . supposed to be; **F:** No, it isn't
6. **L:** are . . . supposed to do; **F:** 're supposed to leave
7. **L:** Is . . . supposed to rain; **F:** No, it isn't
8. **F:** Are . . . supposed to shake

UNIT **35** FUTURE POSSIBILITY:
MAY, MIGHT, COULD

❶

2. may go
3. could be
4. might want
5. may not be
6. might not be
7. could go
8. might not understand
9. might not want to
10. could stay

❷

2. might buy
3. is going to rain
4. is going to see
5. might go
6. is going to work
7. might have
8. is going to call
9. is going to read
10. might write

❸

How are you? It's the Fourth of July, and it's raining really hard. They say it could clear up later. Then again, it c~~oul~~d **might OR may** not. You never know with the weather.

Do you remember my brother, Ed? He says hi. He might h~~as~~ **have** dinner with me on Saturday night. We may go to a new Mexican restaurant that opened in the mall.

I definitely ~~might take~~ **am going to take OR am taking** some vacation next month. Perhaps we could do something together. It might ~~not~~ be fun to do some traveling. What do you think? Let me know.

❹

(Answers will vary.)

UNIT **36** ASSUMPTIONS:
MUST, HAVE (GOT) TO, MAY,
MIGHT, COULD, CAN'T

❶

2. must not be
3. must feel
4. must not have
5. must know
6. must have
7. must not hear
8. must feel
9. must speak
10. must not study
11. must have
12. must not eat

❷

2. might
3. must
4. must
5. might
6. could
7. could
8. must
9. must
10. couldn't

❸

2. She must
3. They must
4. He must be
5. She might
6. It must be
7. They might be
8. She must
9. He might be
10. They must be

❹

2. Could
3. can't
4. Bob
5. Chet
6. could
7. might
8. Dave
9. could
10. couldn't
11. Allen

❺

(Answers will vary)

❻

Just got home. It's really cold outside. The temperature c~~oul~~d **must** be below freezing because the walkway is all covered with ice. What a day! We went down to the police station to look at photos. They must h~~aving~~ **have** hundreds of photos. They kept showing us more and more. We kept looking, but it was difficult to be sure. After all, we only saw the burglar for a few seconds. They've ~~gotta~~ **got to** have other witnesses besides us! There were a lot of people at the mall that day. We ~~may not~~ **can't OR couldn't** be the only ones who got a look at the burglar! That's the one thing I'm certain of! In spite of our uncertainty with the photos, the detective was very patient. I guess he must be used to witnesses like us. Nevertheless, it h~~ave~~ **has** to be frustrating for him. I know the police ~~may~~ **must** really want to catch this guy.

PART VIII NOUNS AND ARTICLES

UNIT **NOUNS AND QUANTIFIERS**

❶

Proper nouns: Election Day, Japanese, Richard, Yeltsin

Common count nouns: chair, class, country, day, dollar, hamburger, pen, president, snowflake, story, zoo

Common non-count nouns: biology, furniture, honesty, ink, money, news, rice, snow, spaghetti, sugar, swimming

❷

2. Potatoes are . . . Rice is
3. Potato chips are
4. Americans eat . . . people
5. kills
6. Popcorn is
7. Peanuts are not
8. Peanut butter has
9. history . . . is
10. Ice cream is

❸

2. many (c.)   6. many (b.)
3. much (b.)   7. much (b.)
4. many (c.)   8. many (a.)
5. much (b.)

❹

2. many   7. some
3. few   8. a few
4. many   9. much
5. much   10. enough
6. Several

❺

(Answers will vary.)

UNIT **ARTICLES: INDEFINITE AND DEFINITE**

❶

1. the . . . the
2. the
3. the
4. the . . . the
5. a . . . The . . . the
6. the
7. Ø . . . Ø
8. the . . . a
9. an . . . a
10. Ø . . . Ø
11. some . . . a . . . the . . . the
12. the . . . a . . . The

❷

2. a   13. the
3. A   14. the
4. a   15. the
5. Ø   16. the
6. Ø   17. the
7. a   18. an
8. Ø   19. Ø
9. The   20. a
10. Ø   21. Ø
11. a   22. the
12. The

❸

2. a   15. an
3. a   16. the
4. the   17. the
5. the   18. The
6. the   19. a
7. the   20. the
8. the   21. the
9. the   22. the
10. The   23. The
11. the   24. the
12. a   25. the
13. the   26. Ø
14. the   27. the

Test: Units 22–25

DIRECTIONS: *Circle the letter of the correct answer to complete each sentence.*

Example:

Jackie never _____ coffee.   **A (B) C D**
   (A) drink   (C) is drinking
   (B) drinks   (D) was drinking

1. I have _____ boss in the world.   **A B C D**
   (A) a good   (C) the best
   (B) best   (D) the better

2. Jessica is an excellent employee. She works   **A B C D**
_____, and she's very dependable.
   (A) as hard   (C) harder than
   (B) hard   (D) hardly

3. The apple pie smells _____.   **A B C D**
   (A) more wonderfully   (C) wonderful
   (B) the most wonderfully (D) wonderfully

4. The larger the apartment, the _____   **A B C D**
the rent.
   (A) expensive   (C) more expensive
   (B) expensively   (D) most expensive

5. That's _____ story I have ever heard.   **A B C D**
   (A) a ridiculous   (C) the more ridiculous
   (B) the ridiculous   (D) the most ridiculous

6. This living room isn't as _____ ours.   **A B C D**
   (A) big as   (C) bigger than
   (B) bigger   (D) biggest

7. Stella drives more _____ Phil.   A B C D
   (A) careful as   (C) careful than
   (B) carefully as   (D) carefully than

8. Is there anything else on TV? This show doesn't seem _____.   A B C D
   (A) interested   (C) interestingly
   (B) interesting   (D) more interested

9. Riding in a car is more dangerous _____ flying.   A B C D
   (A) as   (C) than
   (B) from   (D) that

10. Please call if you're going to arrive _____.   A B C D
   (A) as late   (C) lately
   (B) late   (D) later than

11. It's getting more and _____ to find a cheap apartment.   A B C D
   (A) difficult   (C) more difficult
   (B) less difficult   (D) more difficult than

12. She plays the piano _____ as she sings.   A B C D
   (A) as beautiful   (C) more beautifully
   (B) as beautifully   (D) the most beautifully

PART TWO

DIRECTIONS: _Each sentence has four underlined words or phrases._
The four underlined parts of the sentence are marked A, B, C, and D.
Circle the letter of the one underlined word or phrase that is NOT
CORRECT.

Example:

Ana <u>rarely</u> <u>is drinking</u> coffee, but <u>this morning</u> she <u>is having</u> a cup.   A Ⓑ C D
      A   B   C   D

13. Today will be <u>colder,</u> <u>wetter,</u> and <u>windier</u> <u>that</u> yesterday.   A B C D
                A   B   C   D

14. This <u>nice</u> <u>new</u> apartment looks <u>perfectly</u> for a <u>young</u> couple.   A B C D
        A B   C   D

15. Our <u>new</u> telephone answering machine doesn't operate as <u>quiet</u> <u>as</u>   A B C D
      A   B   C

   our <u>old</u> one.
       D

16. The clothes at Brooks are <u>nicer,</u> <u>interesting,</u> and <u>less expensive</u> <u>than</u>   A B C D
                                A   B   C   D

   the clothes at B & S Department Store.

17. This is the <u>more interesting</u> and the <u>funniest</u> book I have <u>ever</u> <u>read</u>.   A B C D
               A   B   C D

18. Thompson controlled the ball <u>the best</u>, kicked the ball <u>the farthest</u>,
                            A   B   **A B C D**
and ran the <u>faster</u> <u>of</u> all the players.
                  C   D

19. The critic was <u>amused</u> by the <u>funny</u> story line, but she found the   **A B C D**
                              A   B
acting <u>extremely</u> <u>unexcited</u>.
          C   D

20. It's getting <u>easy</u> and <u>easier</u> to find a <u>good</u> <u>inexpensive</u> color TV.   **A B C D**
               A   B   C   D

TEST: UNITS 26–31

T4

PART ONE

DIRECTIONS: Circle the letter of the correct answer to complete each sentence.

Example:

Jackie never _____ coffee.   A (B) C D

   (A) drink   (C) is drinking
   (B) drinks   (D) was drinking

1. Do you enjoy _____?   A B C D
   (A) swim   (C) the swimming
   (B) swimming   (D) to swim

2. I'm looking forward to _____ on vacation.   A B C D
   (A) be going   (C) going
   (B) go   (D) have gone

3. The doctor advised Mike to stop _____.   A B C D
   (A) for smoking   (C) smoking
   (B) smoke   (D) to smoke

4. She's going on a diet in order _____ weight.   A B C D
   (A) for not gaining   (C) not to gain
   (B) not for gaining   (D) to gain not

5. I'm excited _____ starting my new job.   A B C D
   (A) about   (C) of
   (B) for   (D) to

6. Maria is not used to _____ alone.   A B C D
   (A) live   (C) lived
   (B) lives   (D) living

7. Have you ever considered _____ jobs?   A B C D
   (A) change   (C) changing
   (B) changed   (D) to change

8. Where did he use to _____? A B C D
   (A) live   (C) lives
   (B) lived   (D) living

9. Meng is interested _____ to college. A B C D
   (A) for going   (C) to go
   (B) in going   (D) to going

PART TWO

DIRECTIONS: Each sentence has four underlined words or phrases. The four underlined parts of the sentence are marked A, B, C, and D. Circle the letter of the <u>one</u> underlined word or phrase that is NOT CORRECT.

Example:

Ana <u>rarely is drinking</u> coffee, but <u>this morning</u> she <u>is having</u> a cup. A (B) C D
     A   B   C   D

10. <u>Collecting</u> <u>stamps</u> <u>are</u> <u>a</u> popular hobby. A B C D
     A   B   C D

11. Bo needs a ladder because he's <u>not</u> <u>enough tall</u> <u>to</u> <u>reach</u> the shelf. A B C D
                                 A   B   C D

12. When <u>do</u> you <u>expect</u> <u>him</u> <u>being</u> here? A B C D
          A   B   C   D

13. <u>Before</u> <u>leaving</u> the office, please <u>remember</u> <u>locking</u> the door. A B C D
     A B   C   D

14. Fran <u>enjoys</u> <u>dancing</u> and looks forward <u>to</u> <u>learn</u> the latest dances. A B C D
         A   B   C D

15. After <u>moving</u> to Canada, Monica had to get <u>used</u> <u>to</u> <u>do</u> everything A B C D
       A   B C D
   in English.

16. Sue was so excited <u>about</u> <u>winning</u> the contest that she <u>forgot</u> A B C D
                     A   B   C
   <u>meeting</u> her husband at the restaurant.
      D

17. Scott <u>didn't run</u> fast <u>enough</u> <u>for</u> <u>win</u> the race. A B C D
          A   B   C D

18. Erica <u>avoids</u> <u>going</u> <u>to</u> parties because she has trouble <u>to remember</u> A B C D
         A   B C   D
   people's names.

19. <u>To do</u> sit-ups <u>is</u> hard work, and many people don't <u>enjoy</u> <u>doing</u> them. A B C D
     A   B   C   D

20. Jimmy's father forced <u>him</u> <u>to apologize</u> <u>of</u> <u>breaking</u> the window. A B C D
                       A   B   C   D

TEST: UNITS 32–36

PART ONE

DIRECTIONS: *Circle the letter of the correct answer to complete each sentence.*

Example:

Jackie never _____ coffee.   A (B) C D
    (A) drink   (C) is drinking
    (B) drinks   (D) was drinking

1. According to the law, everyone must   A B C D
   _____ a license in order to drive.
   (A) has   (C) have to
   (B) have   (D) to have

2. _____ rain tomorrow?   A B C D
   (A) Is it going to   (C) Should it
   (B) May it   (D) Would it

3. I _____ arrive on time, so please start   A B C D
   dinner without me.
   (A) could   (C) may not
   (B) may   (D) should

4. Jamie prefers working at home _____   A B C D
   working in an office.
   (A) more   (C) that
   (B) than   (D) to

5. You _____ forget to pay your taxes.   A B C D
   (A) don't have to   (C) must
   (B) have to   (D) must not

6. According to the weather forecast, there   A B C D
   _____ some rain tomorrow.
   (A) could   (C) may be
   (B) may   (D) maybe

7. It's dark out. It _____ be late.   **A B C D**
   (A) could   (C) must
   (B) might   (D) ought to

8. **A:** Is Doug an exchange student?   **A B C D**
   B: I'm not sure. He _____.
   (A) could   (C) must not be
   (B) couldn't   (D) could be

9. When _____ you supposed to call Matt?   **A B C D**
   (A) do   (C) must
   (B) are   (D) should

10. You _____ buy a gift, but you can if you want to.   **A B C D**
    (A) have to   (C) must
    (B) don't have to   (D) must not

11. **A:** _____ the package arrive tomorrow?   **A B C D**
    B: It might. I mailed it two days ago.
    (A) Could   (C) May
    (B) Do you prefer   (D) Must

12. **A:** Do you think Warren is over twenty?   **A B C D**
    B: He _____ be. I've known him for more than twenty
        years!
    (A) could   (C) might
    (B) has to   (D) must not

13. **A:** Are you going to the party tonight?   **A B C D**
    B: I _____. I'm pretty tired.
    (A) could   (C) 'd prefer to
    (B) don't like to   (D) might not

PART TWO

DIRECTIONS: Each sentence has four underlined words or phrases.
The four underlined parts of the sentence are marked A, B, C, and D.
Circle the letter of the <u>one</u> underlined word or phrase that is NOT
CORRECT.

Example:

Ana <u>rarely</u> <u>is drinking</u> coffee, but <u>this morning</u> she <u>is having</u> a cup.   **A Ⓑ C D**
     A   B   C   D

14. <u>I'd</u> rather <u>having</u> dinner at home <u>than</u> <u>eat</u> out.   **A B C D**
   A   B   C D

15. My sister <u>may</u> <u>arrives</u> before <u>I can</u> <u>get</u> to the train station.   **A B C D**
         A   B   C D

16. Why <u>do</u> you <u>prefer</u> newspapers <u>than</u> magazines<u>?</u>   **A B C D**
       A   B   C   D

17. Jared <u>will be</u> <u>supposed</u> <u>to be</u> there tomorrow, but he <u>can't</u> go.   **A B C D**
           A   B   C   D

18. It <u>must</u> rain <u>tonight</u>, so I <u>prefer</u> <u>to stay</u> home.   **A B C D**
         A   B   C   D

19. You <u>don't have to</u> <u>drive</u> so fast or you <u>could</u> <u>get</u> a ticket.   **A B C D**
            A   B   C D

20. Everyone <u>have to</u> <u>come</u> on time unless <u>they'd rather</u> <u>miss</u> the   **A B C D**
             A   B   C   D

opening speech.

TEST: UNITS 37–38

DIRECTIONS: *Circle the letter of the correct answer to complete each sentence. Use Ø when no word is needed.*

Example:

Jackie never ʻ_____ coffee.   A Ⓑ C D

   (A) drink   (C) is drinking
   (B) drinks   (D) was drinking

1. _____ the mail arrived yet?   A B C D

   (A) Are   (C) Has
   (B) Is   (D) Have

2. She was unhappy because _____ of her   A B C D
friends sent her birthday cards.

   (A) a few   (C) few
   (B) a little   (D) little

3. They didn't have _____ shoes in my size.   A B C D

   (A) a great deal of   (C) much
   (B) a lot of   (D) some

4. Can you lend me _____ money?   A B C D

   (A) little   (C) many
   (B) some   (D) a few

5. _____ university is larger than a college.   A B C D

   (A) A   (C) The
   (B) An   (D) Ø

6. That's _____ best story I've ever heard.   A B C D

   (A) a   (C) the
   (B) an   (D) Ø

7. _____ music is Jane's favorite pastime.   A B C D

   (A) A   (C) The
   (B) An   (D) Ø

8. You have to protect your skin from _____ sun.   A B C D
    (A) a   (C) the
    (B) an   (D) Ø

9. Pauline doesn't eat _____ spaghetti.   A B C D
    (A) much   (C) the
    (B) many   (D) a few

10. **A:** What does David do?   A B C D
    B: He's _____ accountant.
    (A) a   (C) the
    (B) an   (D) Ø

11. Can you turn on _____ TV? I want to watch the news.   A B C D
    (A) a   (C) the
    (B) an   (D) Ø

12. **A:** I rented _____ video last night.   A B C D
    B: Oh? Which one?
    (A) a   (C) the
    (B) an   (D) Ø

PART TWO

DIRECTIONS: Each sentence has four underlined words or phrases. The four underlined parts of the sentence are marked A, B, C, and D. Circle the letter of the <u>one</u> underlined word or phrase that is NOT CORRECT.

Example:

Ana <u>rarely</u> <u>is drinking</u> coffee, but <u>this morning</u> she <u>is having</u> a cup.   A Ⓑ C D
    A   B   C   D

13. <u>The</u> news <u>were</u> very sad, and everyone <u>was</u> talking about <u>it</u>.   A B C D
     A   B   C   D

14. Jackie <u>has</u> been <u>a</u> honor student ever since she began her <u>studies</u> at   A B C D
            A   B   C
    <u>the university</u>.
       D

15. I need <u>some advice</u> about what to bring to my <u>aunt's</u> house on   A B C D
           A   B
    <u>thanksgiving</u> next <u>Thursday</u>.
       C   D

16. How <u>many</u> times do I have to tell you not to leave <u>your</u> wet <u>shoes</u>   A B C D
         A   B   C
    on <u>a</u> kitchen floor?
       D

17. Mathematics <u>are</u> Sally's favorite school <u>subject</u>, and she always <u>gets</u>   A B C D
              A   B   C
    high <u>grades</u>.
        D

18. I have <u>a little</u> money, so I can't take <u>a</u> vacation until <u>next</u> year at <u>the</u>   **A B C D**

      A   B   C   D

    earliest.

19. We need to pick up <u>some sugar</u> and <u>banana</u> at <u>the</u> supermarket on   **A B C D**

                 A   B   C

    <u>the</u> way home.

     D

20. Pat turned on <u>the</u> TV in order to see <u>the</u> weather report on <u>an</u>   **A B C D**

              A   B   C

    evening <u>news</u>.

         D

Answer Key for Tests

Note: Correct responses for Part Two questions appear in parentheses ( ).

Answer Key for Test: UNITS 22–25

Part One
1.	C	7.	D
2.	B	8.	B
3.	C	9.	C
4.	C	10.	B
5.	D	11.	C
6.	A	12.	B

Part Two
13. D (than)
14. C (perfect)
18. C (fastest)
15. B (quietly)
16. B (more interesting)
17. A (most interesting)
19. D (unexciting)
20. A (easier)

Answer Key for Test: UNITS 26–31

Part One
1.	B	6.	D
2.	C	7.	C
3.	C	8.	A
4.	C	9.	B
5.	A		

Part Two
10. C (is)
11. B (tall enough)
12. D (to be)
13. D (to lock)
14. D (learning)
15. D (doing)
16. D (to meet)
17. C (to)
18. D (remembering)
19. A (Doing)
20. C (for)

Answer Key for Test: UNITS 32–36

Part One
1.	B	8.	D
2.	A	9.	B
3.	C	10.	B
4.	D	11.	A
5.	D	12.	B
6.	C	13.	D
7.	C		

Part Two
14. B (have)
15. B (arrive)
16. C (to)
17. A (is OR was)
18. A (might OR could)
19. A (must not OR 'd better not)
20. A (has to)

Answer Key for Test: UNITS 37–38

Part One
1.	C	7.	D
2.	C	8.	C
3.	B	9.	A
4.	B	10.	B
5.	A	11.	C
6.	C	12.	A

Part Two
13. B (was)
14. B (an)
15. C (Thanksgiving)
16. D (the)
17. A (is)
18. A (little)
19. B (bananas)
20. C (the)